THE TINDER-BOX

Maria Thompson Daviess

1st WORLD LIBRARY Literary Society

The Tinder-Box

Maria Thompson Daviess

© 1st World Library, 2006
PO Box 2211
Fairfield, IA 52556
www.1stworldlibrary.com
First Edition

LCCN: 2006907716

Softcover ISBN: 1-4218-2444-2
Hardcover ISBN: 1-4218-2344-6
eBook ISBN: 1-4218-2544-9

Purchase *"Tinder-Box"*
as a traditional bound book at:
www.1stWorldLibrary.com/purchase.asp?ISBN=1-4218-2444-2

1st World Library is a literary, educational organization
dedicated to:

- Creating a free internet library of downloadable ebooks

- Hosting writing competitions and offering book
publishing scholarships.

Interested in more 1st World Library books?
contact: literacy@1stworldlibrary.com
Check us out at: www.1stworldlibrary.com

1st World Library Literary Society

Giving Back to the World

"If you want to work on the core problem, it's early school literacy."

- James Barksdale, former CEO of Netscape

"No skill is more crucial to the future of a child, or to a democratic and prosperous society, than literacy."

- Los Angeles Times

Literacy... means far more than learning how to read and write... The aim is to transmit... knowledge and promote social participation."

- UNESCO

"Literacy is not a luxury, it is a right and a responsibility. If our world is to meet the challenges of the twenty-first century we must harness the energy and creativity of all our citizens."

- President Bill Clinton

"Parents should be encouraged to read to their children, and teachers should be equipped with all available techniques for teaching literacy, so the varying needs and capacities of individual kids can be taken into account."

- Hugh Mackay

CONTENTS

CHAPTER I

THE LOAD

All love is a gas, and it takes either loneliness, strength of character, or religion to liquefy it into a condition to be ladled out of us, one to another. There is a certain dangerously volatile state of it; and occasionally people, especially of opposite sexes, try to administer it to each other in that form, with asphyxiation resulting to both hearts. And I'm willing to confess that it is generally a woman's fault when such an accident occurs. That is, it is a mistake of her nature, not one of intent. But she is learning!

Also when a woman is created, the winds have wooed star-dust, rose-dew, peach-down, and a few flint-shavings into a whirlwind of deviltry, and the world at large looks on in wonder and sore amazement, as well as breathless interest. I know, because I am one, and have just been waked up by the gyrations of the cyclone; and I'm deeply confounded. I don't like it, and wish I could have slept longer, but Fate and Jane Mathers decreed otherwise. At least Jane decreed, and Fate seems so far helpless to controvert the decree.

I might have known that when this jolly, easy-going old Fate of mine, which I inherited from a lot of indolent, pleasure-loving Harpeth Valley Tennesseans, let me pack up my graduating thesis, my B.S., and some delicious frocks, and go off to Paris for a degree from the Beaux Arts in Architecture, we would be caught up with by some kind of Nemesis or other, and put in our place in the biological and ethnological scheme of existence. Yes, Fate and I are placed, and Jane did it.

Also, I am glad, now that I know what is going to happen to me, that I had last week on shipboard, with Richard Hall bombarding my cardiac regions with his honest eyes and booming voice discreetly muffled to accord with the moonlight and the quiet places around the deck. I may never get that sort of a joy-drink again, but it was so well done that it will help me to administer the same to others when the awful occasion arrives.

"A woman is the spark that lights the flame on the altar of the inner man, dear, and you'll have to sparkle when your time comes," he warned me, as I hurried what might have been a very tender parting, the last night at sea.

"*Spark*" - she's a conflagration by this new plan of Jane's, but I'm glad he didn't know about it then. He may have to suffer from it yet. It is best for him to be as happy as he can as long as he can.

"Evelina, dear," said Jane, as she and Mary Elizabeth Conners and I sat in the suite of apartments in which our proud Alma Mater had lodged us old grads, returned for our second degrees, "your success has been remarkable, and I am not surprised at all that that positively creative thesis of yours on the Twentieth Century Garden, to which I listened to-night, procured you an honorable mention in your class at the Beaux Arts. The French are a nation that quickly recognizes genius. I am very happy to-night. All your honors and achievements make me only the more certain that I have chosen the right person for the glorious mission I am about to offer you."

Maria Thompson Daviess

"Oh, no, Jane!" I exclaimed, from a sort of instinct for trouble to come. I know that devoted, twenty-second century look in Jane's intense, near-sighted eyes, and I always fend from it. She is a very dear person, and I respectfully adore her. Indeed, I sometimes think she is the real spine in my back that was left out of me, and of its own strength got developed into another and a finer woman. She became captain of my Freshman soul, at the same time she captured the captaincy of the boat crew, on which I pulled stroke, and I'm still hitting the water when she gives the word, though it now looks as if we are both adrift on the high and uncharted seas - or sitting on the lid of a tinder-box, juggling lighted torches.

"You see, dear," she went on to say slowly, drawing Mary Elizabeth into the spell-bound circle of our intensity, as we three sat together with our newly-engraved sheepskins on our knees, "for these two years while you have been growing and developing along all your natural lines in a country which was not your own, in a little pool I should call it, out of even sight and sound of the current of events, we have been here in your own land engaged in the great work of the organization and reorganization which is molding the destinies of the women of our times, and those that come after us. That is what I want to talk to you about, and devoutly have I been praying that your heart will be receptive to the call that has claimed the life of Mary Elizabeth and me. There is a particular work, for which you are fitted as no other woman I have ever known is fitted, and I want to lay the case plainly before you to-night. Will you give me a hearing?"

And the hearing I gave that beloved and devout woman was the *reveille* that awakened me to this - this whirlwind that seems to be both inside me and outside me, and everywhere else in the whole world.

It's not woman's suffrage; it has gone way down past the road from votes for women. I wish I could have stopped in that political field of endeavor before Jane got to me. She might have left me there doing little things like making speeches before the United States Senate and running for Governor of Tennessee, after I had, single-handed, remade the archaic constitution of that proud and bat-blind old State of my birth; but such ease was not for me.

Of course for years, as all women have been doing who are sensible enough to use the brains God gave them and stop depending on their centuries-seasoned intuitions and fascinations, I have been reading about this feminist revolution that seems all of a sudden to have revoluted from nobody knows where, and I have been generally indignant over things whether I understood them or not, and I have felt that I was being oppressed by the opposite sex, even if I could not locate the exact spot of the pain produced. I have always felt that when I got to it I would shake off the shackles of my queer fondness and of my dependence upon my oppressors, and do something revengeful to them.

When my father died in my Junior year and left me all alone in the world, the first thing that made me feel life in my veins again was the unholy rage I experienced when I found that he had left me bodaciously and otherwise to my fifth cousin, James Hardin.

Cousin James is a healthy reversion to the primitive type of Father Abraham, and he has so much aristo-cratic moss on him that he reminds me of that old gray crag that hangs over Silver Creek out on Providence Road. Artistically he is perfectly beautiful in an Old-Testament fashion. He lives in an ancient, rambling house across the road from my home, and he is making a souvenir collection of

Maria Thompson Daviess

derelict women. Everybody that dies in Glendale leaves him a relict, and including his mother, Cousin Martha, he now has either seven or nine female charges, depending on the sex of Sallie Carruthers's twin babies, which I can't exactly remember, but will wager is feminine.

My being left to him was an insult to me, though of course Father did not see it that way. He adored the Crag, as everybody else in Glendale does, and wouldn't have considered not leaving him precious me. Wanting to ignore Cousin James, because I was bound out to him until my twenty-fifth year or marriage, which is worse, has kept me from Glendale all these four years since father died suddenly while I was away at college, laid up with the ankle which I broke in the gymnasium. Still, as much as I resent him, I keep the letter the Crag wrote me the night after Father died, right where I can put my hand on it if life suddenly panics me for any reason. It covers all the circumstances I have yet met. I wonder if I ought to burn it now!

But, to be honest with myself, I will have to confess that the explosively sentimental scene on the front porch, the night I left for college, with Polk Hayes has had something to do with my cowardice in lingering in foreign climes. I feel that it is something I will have to go on with some day, and the devil will have to pick up the chips. Polk is the kind of man that ought to be exterminated by the government in sympathy for its women wards, if his clan didn't make such good citizens when they do finally marry. He ought at least to be labeled "poison for the very young." I was very young out on the porch that night. Still, I don't resent him like I do the archaic Crag.

And as Jane talked, my seasoned indignation of four years against my keeper flared up, and while she paused at intervals for breath I hurled out plans for his demolishment. I wish now I had been more conservatively quiet, and left myself a loophole, but I didn't. I walked into this situation and shut the door behind me.

"Yes, Evelina, I think you will have to insist forcibly on assuming charge of your own social and financial affairs in your own home. It may not be easy, with such a man as you describe, but you will accomplish it. However, many mediocre women have proved their ability to attend to their own fortunes, and do good business for themselves; but your battle is to be fought on still higher grounds. You are to rise and establish with your fellow-man a plane of common citizenship. You do it for his sake and your own, and for that of humanity."

"Suppose, after I get up there on that plateau, I didn't find any man at all," I ventured faint-heartedly, but with a ripple of my risibles; the last in life I fear.

"You must reach down your hands to them and draw them up to you," she answered in a tone of tonic inspiration. "You are to claim the same right to express your emotions that a man has. You are to offer your friendship to both men and women on the same frank terms, with no degrading hesitancy caused by an embarrassment on account of your sex. It is his due and yours. No form of affection is to be withheld from him. It is to be done frankly and impressively, and when the time comes - " I can hardly write this, but the memory of the wonderful though fanatic light in Jane's eyes makes me able to scrawl it - "that you feel the mating instinct in you move towards any man, I charge you that you are to consider it a sacred obligation to express it with the same honesty that a man would express the same thing to you, in like case, even if he has shown no sign of that impulse toward you. No contortions and contemptible indirect method of

Maria Thompson Daviess

attack, but a fearless one that is yours by right, and his though he may not acknowledge it. The barbaric and senseless old convention that denies women the right of selection, for which God has given her the superior instinct, is to be broken down by just such women as you. A woman less dowered by beauty and all feminine charm could not do it just yet, but to you, to whom the command of men is a natural gift, is granted the wonderful chance to prove that it can be done, honestly and triumphantly, with no sacrifice of the sacredness of womanhood."

"Oh, Jane." I moaned into the arm of the chair on which I had bowed my head.

I am moaning; now just as much, down in the bottom of my heart. Where are all my gentle foremothers that smiled behind their lace fans and had their lily-white hands kissed by cavalier gentlemen in starched ruffles, out under the stars that rise over Old Harpeth, that they don't claim me in a calm and peaceful death? Still, as much as I would like to die, I am interested in what is going to happen.

"Yes, Evelina," she answered in an adamant tone of voice, "and when I have the complete record of what, I know, will be your triumphant vindication of the truth that it is possible and advisable for women to assert their divine right to choose a mate for their sacred vocation of bearing the race, I shall proceed, as I have told you, to choose five other suitable young women to follow your example, and furnish them the money, up to the sum of a hundred thousand dollars, after having been convinced by your experience. Be careful to make the most minute records, of even the most emotional phases of the question, in this book for their guidance. Of course, they will never know the source of the data, and I will help you elucidate and arrange the book, after it is all accomplished."

If Jane hadn't had two million dollars all this trouble would not be.

"I can never do it!" I exclaimed with horror, "And the men will hate it - and me. And if I did do it, I couldn't write it."

I almost sobbed as a vision flashed before me of thus verbally snap-shotting the scene with dear old Dickie as we stood against the rail of the ship and watched the waves fling back silvery radiance at the full moon, and I also wondered how I was to render in serviceable written data his husky:

"A woman is the flame that lights the spark - "

Also, what would that interview with Polk Hayes look like reproduced with high lights?

"Now," she answered encouragingly, "don't fear the men, dear. They are sensible and business-like creatures, and they will soon see how much to their advantage it is to be married to women who have had an equal privilege with themselves of showing their preferences. Then only can they be sure that their unions are from real preferences and not compromises, on the part of their wives, from lack of other choice. Of course, a woman's pride will make her refrain from courtship, as does her brother man, until she is financially independent, and self-supporting, lest she be put in the position of a mendicant." Jane has thought the whole thing out from Genesis to Revelation.

Still, that last clause about the mendicant leaves hope for the benighted man who still wants the cling of the vine. A true vine would never want - or be able - to hustle enough to flower sordid dollars instead of curls and blushes.

"A woman would have to be - to be a good deal of a woman, not any less one, to put such a thing across, Jane," I said, with a preflash of some of the things that might happen in such a cruel crusade of reformation and deprivation of rights.

"That is the reason I have chosen you to collect the data, Evelina," answered Jane, with another of those glorious tonic looks, issuing from my backbone in her back. "The ultimate woman must be superb in body, brain, and heart. You are that now more nearly than any one I have ever seen. You are the woman!"

I was silenced with awe.

"Jane plans to choose five girls who would otherwise have to spend their lives teaching in crowded cities after leaving college and to start them in any profession they choose, with every chance of happiness, in the smaller cities of the South and Middle West," said Mary Elizabeth gently, and somehow the tears rose in my eyes, as I thought how the poor dear had been teaching in the high school in Chicago the two glorious years I had been frolicking abroad. No time, and no men to have good times with.

And there were hundreds like her, I knew, in all the crowded parts of the United States. And as I had begun, I thought further. Just because I was embarrassed at the idea of proposing to some foolish man, who is of no importance to me, himself, or the world in general, down in Glendale, where they have all known me all my life, and would expect anything of me anyway after I have defied tradition and gone to college, five lovely, lonely girls would have to go without any delightful suitors like Richard - or Polk Hayes, forever.

And, still further, I thought of the other girls, coming under the influence of those five, who might be encouraged to hold up their heads and look around, and at least help out their Richards in their matrimonial quest, and as I sat there with Jane's compelling and Mary Elizabeth's hungry eyes on me, I felt that I was being besought by all the lovers of all the future generations to tear down some sort of awful barrier and give them happiness. And it was the thought of the men that was most appealing. It takes a woman who really likes them as I do, and has their good really at heart, to see their side of the question as Jane put it, poor dears. Suddenly, I felt that all the happiness of the whole world was in one big, golden chalice, and that I had to hold it steadily to give drink to all men and all women - with a vision of little unborn kiddies in the future.

Then, before I could stop myself, I decided - and I hope the dear Lord - I say it devoutly - indeed I do! - will help that poor man in Glendale if I pick out the wrong one. I'm going to do it.

"I accept your appointment and terms, Jane," I said quietly, as I looked both those devout, if fanatic, women in the face. "I pledge myself to go back to Glendale, to live a happy, healthy, normal life, as useful as I can make it. I had intended to do that anyway, for if I am to evolve the real American garden. I can't do better than sketch and study those in the Harpeth Valley, for at least two seasons all around. I shall work at my profession whole-heartedly, take my allotted place in the community, and refuse to recognize any difference in the obligations and opportunities in my life and that of the men with whom I am thrown, and to help all other women to take such a fearless and honest attitude - if Glendale blows up in consequence. I will seek and claim marriage in exactly the same fearless way a man does, and when I have found what I want I shall expect you to put one hundred thousand dollars, twenty to each, at the disposal of five other suitable young women, to follow my example, as noted down in this book - if it has been successful. Shall I give you some sort of written agreement?"

"Just record the agreement as a note in the book, and I will sign it," answered Jane, in her crispest and most business-like tone of voice, though I could see she was trembling with excitement, and poor Mary Elizabeth was both awe-struck and hopeful.

I'll invite Mary Elizabeth down to Glendale, as soon as I stake out my own claim, poor dear!

And here I sit alone at midnight, with a huge, steel-bound, lock-and-keyed book that Jane has had made for me, with my name and the inscription, "In case of death, send unopened to Jane Mathers, Boston, Massachusetts," on the back, committed to a cause as crazy and as serious as anything since the Pilgrimages, or the Quest of the Knights for the Grail. It also looks slightly like trying to produce a modern Don Quixote, feminine edition, and my cheeks are flaming so that I wouldn't look at them for worlds. And to write it all, too! I have always had my opinion of women who spill their souls out of an ink-bottle, but I ought to pardon a nihilist, that in the dead of night, cold with terror, confides some awful appointment he has had made him, to his nearest friend. I am the worst nihilist that ever existed, and the bomb I am throwing may explode and destroy the human race. But, on the other hand, the explosion might be of another kind. Suppose that suddenly a real woman's entire nature should be revealed to the world, might not the universe be enveloped in a rose glory and a love symphony? We'll see!

Also, could the time ever come when a woman wouldn't risk hanging over the ragged edge of Heaven to hold on to the hand of some man? Never! Then, as that is the case, I see we must all keep the same firm grip on the creatures we have always had, and haul them over the edge, but we must not do it any more without letting them know about it - it isn't honest. Yes, women must solidify their love into such a concrete form that men can weigh and measure it, and decide for themselves whether they want to - to climb to Heaven for it, or remain comfortable old bachelors. We mustn't any more lead them into marriage blinded by the overpowering gaseous fragrance called romantic love.

But, suppose I should lose all love for everybody in this queer quest for enlightenment I have undertaken? Please, God, let a good man be in Glendale, Tennessee, who will understand and protect me - no, that's the wrong prayer! Protect him - no - both of us!

Maria Thompson Daviess

CHAPTER II

THE MAIDEN LANCE

A woman may shut her eyes, and put a man determinedly out of her heart, and in two minutes she will wake up in an agony of fear that he isn't there. Now, as I have decided that Glendale is to be the scene of this bloodless revolution of mine - it would be awful to carry out such an undertaking anywhere but under the protection of ancestral traditions - I have operated Richard Hall out of my inmost being with the utmost cruelty, on an average of every two hours, for this week Jane and I have been in New York; and I have still got him with me.

I, at last, became determined, and chose the roof-garden at the Astor to tell him good-by, and perform the final operation. First I tried to establish a plane of common citizenship with him, by telling him how much his two years' friendship across the waters had meant to me, while we studied the same profession under the same masters, drew at the same drawing-boards and watched dear old Paris flame into her jeweled night-fire from Montmarte, together. I was frankly affectionate, and it made him suspicious of me.

Then I tried to tell him just a little, only a hint, of my new attitude towards his sex, and before he had had time even to grasp the idea he exploded.

"Don't talk to me as if you were an alienist trying to examine an abstruse case, Evelina," he growled, with extreme temper. "Go on down and rusticate with your relatives for the summer, and fly the bats in your belfry at the old moss-backs, while I am getting this Cincinnati and Gulf Stations commission under way. Then, when I can, I will come for you. Let's don't discuss the matter, and it's time I took you back to your hotel."

Not a very encouraging tilt for my maiden lance.

I've had a thought. If I should turn and woo Dickie, like he does me, I suppose we would be going-so fast in opposite directions that we would be in danger of passing each other without recognizing signals. I wonder if that might get to be the case of humanity at large if women do undertake the tactics I am to experiment with, and a dearth of any kind of loving and claiming at all be the result. I will elucidate that idea and shoot it into Jane. But I have no hope; she'll have the answer ticketed away in the right pigeon-hole, statistics and all, ready to fire back at me.

I have a feeling that Jane won't expect such a diary as this locked cell of a book is becoming, but I can select what looks like data for the young from these soul squirmings, and only let her have those for The Five. I don't know which are which now, and I'll have to put down the whole drama.

And my home-coming last night was a drama that had in it so much comedy, dashed with tragedy, that I'm a little breathless over it yet. Jane, and my mind is breathing unevenly still.

Considering the situation, and my intentions, I was a bit frightened as the huge engine rattled and roared its way

Maria Thompson Daviess

along the steel rails that were leading me back, down into the Harpeth Valley. But, when we crossed the Kentucky line, I forgot the horrors of my mission, and I thrilled gloriously at getting hack to my hills. Old Harpeth had just come into sight, as we rounded into the valley and Providence Knob rested back against it, in a pink glow that I knew came from the honeysuckle in bloom all over it like a mantle. I traveled fast into the twilight, and I saw all the stars smile out over the ridge, in answer to the hearth stars in the valley, before I got across Silver Creek. I hadn't let any one know that I was coming, so I couldn't expect any one to meet me at the station at Glendale. There was nobody there I belonged to - just an empty house. I suppose a man coming home like that would have whistled and held up his head, but I couldn't. I'm a woman.

Suddenly, that long glowworm of a train stopped just long enough at Glendale to eject me and my five trunks, with such hurried emphasis that I felt I was being planted in the valley forever, and I would have to root myself here or die. I still feel that way.

And as I stood just where my feet were planted, in the dust of the road, instead of on the little ten-foot platform, that didn't quite reach to my sleeper steps, I felt as small as I really am in comparison to the universe. I looked after the train and groveled.

Then, just as I was about to start running down the track, away from nowhere and to nowhere, I was brought to my senses by a loud boohoo, and then a snubby choke, which seemed to come out of my bag and steamer-blanket that stood in a pile before me.

"Train's gone, train's gone and left us! I knew it would, when Sallie stopped to put the starch on her face all over again. And Cousin James, he's as slow as molasses, and I couldn't dress two twins in not time to button one baby. Oh, damn, oh, damn!" And the sobs rose to a perfect storm of a wail.

Just at that moment, down the short platform an electric light, that was so feeble that it seemed to show a pine-knot influence in its heredity, was turned on by the station-agent, who was so slow that I perceived the influence of a descent from old Mr. Territt, who drove the stage that came down from the city before the war, and my fellow-sufferer stood revealed.

She was a slim, red-haired bunch of galatea, stylish of cut as to upturned nose and straight little skirt but wholly and defiantly unshod save for a dusty white rag around one pink toe. A cunning little straw bonnet, with an ecru lace jabot dangled in her hand, and her big brown eyes reminded me of Jane's at her most inquisitive moments.

"If you was on a train, what did you git offen it *here* for?" she demanded of me, with both scorn and curiosity in her positive young voice.

"I don't know why," I answered weakly, not at all in the tone of a young-gallant-home-from-the-war mood I had intended to assume towards the first inhabitant of my native town to whom I addressed a remark.

"We was all a-goin' down to Hillsboro, to visit Aunt Bettie Pollard for a whole week, to Cousin Tom's wedding, but my family is too slow for nothing but a funeral. And Cousin James, he's worse. He corned for us ten minutes behind the town clock, and Mammy Dilsie had phthisic, so I had to fix the two twins, and we're done left. I wisht I didn't have no family!" And with her bare feet the young rebel raised a cloud of dust that rose and settled on my skirt.

"There they come now," she continued, with the pained contempt still rising in her voice.

And around the corner of the station hurried the family party, with all the haste they would have been expected to use if they had not, just two minutes earlier, beheld their train go relentlessly on down the valley to Hillsboro and the wedding celebration. I hadn't placed the kiddie, but I might have known, from her own description of her family, to whom she belonged.

First came Sallie Carruthers, sailing along in the serene way that I remembered to have always thought like a swan in no hurry, and in her hands was a wet box from which rose sterns protruded.

Next in the procession came Aunt Dilsie, huge and black and wheezing, fanning herself with a genteel turkey-tail fan, and carrying a large covered basket.

But the tail-piece of the procession paralyzed all the home-coming emotions that I had expected to be feeling, save that of pure hilarity. James Hardin was carrying two bubbly, squirmy, tousle-headed babies, on one arm, and a huge suitcase in the other hand, and his gray felt hat set on the back of his shock of black hair at an angle of deep desperation, though patience shone from every line of his strong, gaunt body, and I could see in the half light that there were no lines of irritation about his mouth, which Richard had said looked to him like that of the prophet Hosea, when I had shown him the picture that Father had had snapped of himself and the Crag, with their great string of quail, on one of their hunting-trips, just before Father died.

"Eve!" he exclaimed, when he suddenly caught sight of me, standing in the middle of the dusty road, with my impedimenta around me, and as he spoke he dropped both babies on the platform in a bunch, and the small trunk on the other side. Then he just stood and looked, and I had to straighten the roar that was arising in me at the sight of him into a conventional smile of greeting, suitable to bestow on an enemy.

But before the smile was well launched, Sallie bustled in and got the full effect of it.

"Why, Evelina Shelby, you darling thing, when did you come?" she fairly bubbled, as she clasped me in the most hospitable of arms, and bestowed a slightly powdery kiss on both my cheeks. I weakly and femininely enjoyed the hug, not that a man might not have - Sallie is a dear, and I always did like her gush, shamefacedly.

"She got offen that train that left us, and she ain't got a bit of sense, or she wouldn't," answered the Blue Bunch for me, in a matter-of-fact tone of voice.

"What for did you all unpack outen the surrey, if you sawed the train go by?" she further demanded, with accusing practicality. "Don't you know when youse left?"

"Oh, Henrietta," exclaimed Sallie, looking at the young-philosopher with terrified helplessness. "Please don't mind her, Evelina. I don't understand her being my child, and nobody does, unless it was Henry's grandmother on his mother's side. You had heard of my loss?"

If I hadn't heard of the death of Henry Carruthers, Sallie's elaborate black draperies, relieved by the filmy exquisiteness of white crepe ruches at the neck and wrists, would have proclaimed the fact.

Suddenly, something made me look at Cousin James, as he stood calmly in the midst of Sallie's family and baggage, both animate and inanimate, and the laugh that had threatened for minutes fairly flared out into his placid, young prophet face.

"Oh, I am so sorry, Sallie, and so glad to see all of you that I'm laughing at the same time," I exclaimed to save myself from the awfulness of greeting a young widow's announcement of her sorrow in such an unfeeling manner. To cover my embarrassment and still further struggles with the laugh that never seemed to be able to have itself out, I bent and hugged up one of the toddlers, who were balancing against the Crag's legs, with truly feminine fervor.

"I'm glad to see you, Evelina," said Cousin James gently, and I could see that the billows of my mirth had got entirely past him.

I was glad he had escaped, and I found myself able to look with composure at his queer, long-tailed gray coat, which made me know that little old Mr. Pinkus, who had been Father's orderly all through the war, was still alive and tailoring in his tiny shop down by the post-office, though now that Father is dead he probably only does it for Cousin James. The two of them had been his only customers for years. And as I looked, I saw that the locks that curled in an ante-bellum fashion around the Crag's ears, were slightly sprinkled with gray, and remembered how he had loved and stood by Father, even in the manner of wearing Pinkus clothes; my heart grew very large all of a sudden, and I held out my hand to him.

"I'm glad to be at home," I said, gazing straight into his eyes, with a look of affection that you would have been proud of, Jane, - using unconsciously, until after I had done it, the warmth I had tried unsuccessfully on Richard Hall at the Astor, not forty-eight hours ago, but two thousand miles away. And it got a response that puzzles me to think of yet. It was just a look, but there was a thought of Father in it, also a suggestion of the glance he bestowed on Sallie's twins. I remembered that the Crag seldom speaks, and that's what makes you spend your time breathlessly listening to him.

"Well, come on, everybody, let's go home and undress, and forget about the wedding," came in Henrietta's positive and executive tones. "Let's go and take the strange lady with us. We can have company if we can't be it. She can sleep other side of me, next the wall."

I have never met anybody else at all like Henrietta Carruthers, and I never shall unless Jane Mathers marries and - I sincerely hope that some day she and Jane will meet.

And the next ten minutes was one of the most strenuous periods of time I ever put in, in all my life. I longed, really longed, to go home with Sallie and Henrietta, and sleep next the wall at Widegables with the rest of the Crag's collection. But I knew Glendale well enough to see plainly that if I thus once give myself up to the conventions that by Saturday night they would have me nicely settled with his relicts, or in my home with probably two elderly widows and a maiden cousin or so to look after me. And then, by the end of the next week, they would have the most suitable person in town fairly hunted by both spoken and mental influence, to the moonlight end of my front porch, with matrimonial intentions in his pocket. I knew I had to take a positive stand, and take it immediately. I must be masculinely firm. No feminine wiles would serve in such a crisis as this.

So, I let Cousin James pack me into his low, prehistoric old surrey, in the front seat, at his side, while Sallie took Aunt Dilsie and one twin with her on the back seat. Henrietta scrouged down at my feet, and I fearingly, but accommodatingly, accepted the other twin. It was a perfect kitten of a baby, and purred itself to sleep against my shoulder as soon as anchored.

The half-mile from the station, along the dusty, quiet village streets, was accomplished in about the time it would take a modern vehicle to traverse Manhattan lengthwise, and at last we stopped at the gate of Widegables. The rambling, winged, wide-gabled, tall-columned old pile of time-grayed brick and stone, sat back in the moonlight, in its tangle of a garden, under its tall roof maples, with a dignity that went straight to my heart. There is nothing better in France or England, and I feel sure that there are not two hundred houses in America as good. I'll paint it, just like I saw it to-night, for next Spring's Salon. A bright light shone from the windows of the dining-room in the left wing, where the collection of clinging vines were taking supper, unconscious of the return of the left-behinds that threatened.

And as I glanced at my own tall-pillared, dark old house, that stands just opposite Widegables, and is of the same period and style, I knew that if I did not escape into its emptiness before I got into Cousin Martha's comfortable arms, surrounded by the rest of the Crag's family, I would never have the courage to enter into the estate of freedom I had planned.

"Sallie," I said firmly, as I handed the limp Kitten down to Aunt Dilsie, as Henrietta took the other one - "Puppy" I suppose I will have to call the young animal, - from her mother and started on up the walk in the lead of the return expedition, "I am going over to stay in my own home to-night. I know it seems strange, but - I *must*. Please don't worry about me."

"Why, dear, you can't stay by yourself, with no man on the place," exclaimed Sallie, in a tone of absolute panic. "I'll go tell Cousin Martha you are here, while Cousin James unpacks your satchel and things." And she hurried in her descent from the ark, and also hurried in her quest for the reinforcement of Cousin Martha's authority.

"I'm going to escape before any of them come back," I said determinedly to the Crag, who stood there still, just looking at me. "I'm not up to arguing the question to-night, for the trip has been a long one, and this is the first time I have been home since - Just let me have to-night to myself, please." I found myself pleading to him, as he held up his arms to lift me clear of the wheels.

His eyes were hurt and suffering for a second, then a strange light of comprehension came from them into mine, like a benediction, as he gently set me on my feet.

"Must you, Eve?"

"Yes," I answered, with a gulp that went all the way down to my feminine toes, as I glanced across the road at the grim, dark old pile that towered against the starlit sky. "I want to stay in my own house to-night - and - and I'm not afraid."

"You won't need to be frightened. I understand, I think - and here's your key, I always carry it in my pocket. Your Father's candle is on the mantel. You shall have to-night to yourself. Good-night, and bless your home-coming, dear!"

"Good-night," I answered as I turned away from his kind

Maria Thompson Daviess

eyes quickly, to keep from clinging-to him with might and main, and crossed the road to my own gate. With my head up, and trying for the whistle, at least in my heart, I went quickly along the front walk with its rows of blush peonies, nodding along either edge. The two old purple lilacs beside the front steps have grown so large they seemed to be barring my way into my home with longing, sweet embraces, and a fragrant little climbing rose, that has rioted across the front door, ever since I could remember, bent down and left a kiss on my cheeks.

The warm, mellow old moon flooded a glow in front of me, through the big front door, as I opened it, and then hastened to pour into the wide windows as I threw back the shutters.

Logs lay ready for lighting in the wide fireplace at the end of the long room, and Father's tobacco jar gleamed a reflected moonlight from its pewter sides from the tall mantel-shelf. The old hooks melted into the dusk of their cases along the wall, and the portrait of Grandfather Shelby lost its fierce gaze and became benign from its place between the windows.

I was being welcomed to the home of my fathers, with a soft dusk that was as still and sweet as the grave. Sweet for those that want it; but I didn't. Suddenly, I thrilled as alive as any terror-stricken woman that ever found herself alone anywhere on any other edge of the world, and then as suddenly found myself in a complete condition of fright prostration, crouched on my own threshold. I was frightened at the dark, and could not even cry. Then almost immediately, while I crouched quivering in every nerve I seemed to hear a man's voice say comfortingly:

"You don't need to be frightened."

Courageously I lifted my eyes and looked down between the old lilac bushes, and saw just what I expected I would, a tall, gray figure, pacing slowly up and down the road. Then it was that fear came into me, stiffened my muscles and strengthened my soul - fear of myself and my own conclusions about destiny and all things pertaining thereto.

I never want to go through such another hour as I spent putting things in order in Father's room, which opens off the living-room, so I could go to bed by candle-light in the bed in which he and I were both born. I wanted to sleep there, and didn't even open any other part of the grim old house.

And when I put out the candle and lay in the high, old four-post bed, I again felt as small as I really am, and I was in danger of a bad collapse from self-depreciation when my humor came to the rescue. I might just as well have gone on and slept between Henrietta and the wall, as was becoming my feminine situation, for here my determination to assert my masculine privileges was keeping a real man doing sentry duty up and down a moonlight road all night - and I wanted it.

"After this, James Hardin, you can consider yourself safe from any of my attentions or intentions," I laughed to myself, as I turned my face into the pillow, that was faintly scented from the lavender in which Mother had always kept her linen. "I've been in Glendale two hours, and one man is on the home base with his fingers crossed. James, you are free! Oh, Jane!"

Maria Thompson Daviess

CHAPTER III

A FLINT SPARK

The greatest upheavals of nature are those that arrive suddenly, without notifying the world days beforehand of their intentions of splitting the crust of the Universe wide open. One is coming to Glendale by degrees, but the town hasn't found out about it yet. I'm the only one who sees it, and I'm afraid to tell.

When Old Harpeth, who has been looking down on a nice, peaceful, man ordained, built, and protected world, woke Glendale up the morning after my arrival and found me defiantly alone in the home of my fathers - also of each of my foremothers, by the courtesy of dower - he muttered and drew a veil of mist across his face. Slight showers ensued, but he had to come out in less than an hour from pure curiosity. I found the old garden heavenly in its riot of neglected buds, shoots, and blooms, wet and welcoming with the soft odors of Heaven itself.

It was well I was out early to enjoy it, for that was to be the day of my temptation and sore trial. I am glad I have recorded it all, for I might have forgotten some day how wonderfully my very pliant, feminine attitude rubbed in my masculine intentions as to my life on the blind side of all the forces brought to bear on me to put me back into my predestined place in the scheme of the existence.

"Your Cousin James's home is the place for you, Evelina, and until he explained to me how you felt last night I was deeply hurt that you hadn't come straight, with Sallie, to me and to him," said Cousin Martha, in as severe a voice as was possible for such a placid individual to produce. Cousin Martha is completely lovely, and the Mossback gets his beauty from her. She is also such a perfect dear that her influence is something terrific, even if negatively expressed.

"I have come to help you get your things together, so you can move over before dinner," she continued with gentle force. "Now, what shall we put in the portmanteau first? I see you have unpacked very little, and I am glad that it confirms me in my feeling that your coming over here for the night was just a dutiful sentiment for your lost loved ones, and not any unmaidenly sense of independence in the matter of choice where it is best for you to live. Of course, such a question as that must be left to your guardian, and of course James will put you under my care."

"I - I really thought that perhaps Cousin James did not have room for me, Cousin Martha," I answered meekly. "How many families has he with him now?" I asked with a still further meekness that was the depths of wiliness.

"There are three of us widows, whom he sustains and comforts for the loss of our husbands, and also the three Norton girls, cousins on his father's side of the house, you remember. It is impossible for them to look after their plantation since their father's death robbed them of a protector, at least, even though he had been paralyzed since Gettysburg. James is a most wonderful man, my dear - a most wonderful man. Though as he is my son I ought to think it in silence."

Maria Thompson Daviess

"Indeed he is," I answered from the heart. "But - but wouldn't it be a little crowded for him to have another - another vine - that is, exactly what would he do with me? I know Widegables is wide, but that is a houseful, isn't it?"

"Well, all of us did feel that it made the house uncomfortably full when Sallie came with the three children, but you know Henry Carruthers left James his executor and guardian of the children, and Sallie of course couldn't live alone, so Mrs. Hargrove and I moved into the south room together, and gave Sallie and the children my room. It is a large room, and it would be such a comfort to Sallie to have you stay with her and help her at night with the children. She doesn't really feel able to get up with them at all. Then Dilsie could sleep in the cabin, as she ought to on account of the jimsonweed in her phthisic pipe. It would be such a beautiful influence in your lonely life, Evelina, to have the children to care for."

I wondered if Cousin Martha had ever heard that galatea bunch indulge in such heartfelt oaths as had followed that train down the track last night!

"It would be lovely," I answered - and the reply was not all insincerity, as I thought of the darkness of that long night, and the Bunch's offer of a place at her sturdy little back "next the wall."

"But I will be so busy with my own work, Cousin Martha, that I am afraid I couldn't do justice to the situation and repay the children and Sallie for crowding them."

"Why, you couldn't crowd us, Evelina, honey," came in Sallie's rich voice, as she sailed into the room, trailing the Pup and the Kit at her skirts and flying lavender ribbons at loose ends. "We've come to help you move over right away."

"Well, not while I have a voice in the affairs of my own husband's niece! How are you, Evelina, and are you crazy, Sallie Carruthers?" came in a deep raven croak of a voice that sounded as if it had harked partly from the tomb, as Aunt Augusta Shelby stood in the doorway, with reproof on her lips and sternness on her brow. "Peter and I will have Evelina move down immediately with us. James Hardin has as much in the way of a family as he can very well stand up under now."

And as she spoke, Aunt Augusta glared at Sallie with such ferocity that even Sallie's sunshiny presence was slightly dimmed.

"Are you ready, Evelina? Peter will send the surrey for your baggage," she continued, and for a moment I quailed, for Aunt Augusta's determination of mind is always formidable, but I summoned my woman's wit and man's courage, and answered quickly before she fairly snatched me from under my own roof-tree.

"That would be lovely, Aunt Augusta, and how are you?" I answered and asked in the same breath, as I drew near enough to her to receive a business-like peck on my cheek. "I expect to have you and Uncle Peter to look after me a lot, but somehow I feel that Father would have liked - liked for me to live here and keep my home - his home - open. Some way will arrange itself. I haven't talked with Cousin James yet," I felt white feathers sprouting all over me, as I thus invoked the masculine dominance I had come to lay.

"You'll have to settle that matter with your Uncle Peter, then, for, following his dictates of which I did not approve, I have done our duty by the orphan. Now,

Evelina, let me say in my own person, that I thoroughly approve of your doing just as you plan." And as she uttered this heresy, she looked so straight and militant and altogether commanding, that both Cousin Martha and Sallie quailed. I felt elated, as if my soul were about to get sight of a kindred personality. Or rather a soul-relative of yours, Jane.

"Oh, she would be so lonely, Mrs. Shelby, and she - " Sallie was venturing to say with trepidation, when Aunt Augusta cut her short without ceremony.

"Lonely, nonsense! Such a busy woman as I now feel sure Evelina is going to be, will not have time to be lonely. I wish I could stay and talk with you further about your plans, but I must hurry back and straighten out Peter's mind on that question of the town water-supply that is to come up in the meeting of the City Council to-day. He let it be presented all wrong last time, and they got things so muddled that it was voted on incorrectly. I will have to write it out for him so he can explain it to them. I will need you in many ways to help me help Peter be Mayor of Glendale, Evelina. I am wearied after ten years of the strain of his office. I shall call on you for assistance often in the most important matters," with which promise, that sounded like a threat, she proceeded to march down the front path, almost stepping on Henrietta, who was coming up the same path, with almost the same emphasis. There was some sort of an explosion, and I hope the kind of words I heard hurled after the train were not used.

"That old black crow is a-going to git in trouble with me some day, Marfy," Henrietta remarked, as she settled herself on the arm of Cousin Martha's chair, after bestowing a smudgy kiss on the little white curl that wrapped around one of the dear old lady's pink little ears. I had felt that way about Cousin Martha myself at the

Bunch's age, and we exchanged a sympathetic smile on the subject.

"Well, what *are* you going to do, Evelina?" asked Sallie, and she turned such a young, helpless, wondering face up to me from the center of her cluster of babies, that my heart almost failed me at the idea of pouring what seemed to me at that moment the poison of modernity into the calm waters of her and Cousin Martha's primitive placidity.

"You'll have to live some place where there is a man," she continued, with worried conviction.

My time had come, and the fight was on. Oh, Jane!

"I don't believe I really feel that way about it," I began in the gentlest of manners, and slowly, so as to feel my way. "You see, Sallie dear, and dearest Cousin Martha, I have had to be out in the world so much - alone, that I am - used to it. I - I haven't had a man's protection for so long that I don't need it, as I would if I were like you two blessed sheltered women."

"I know it has been hard, dear," said Cousin Martha gently looking her sympathy at my lorn state, over her glasses.

"I don't see how you have stood it at all," said Sallie, about to dissolve in tears. "The love and protection and sympathy of a man are the only things in life worth anything to a woman. Since my loss I don't know what I would have done without Cousin James. You must come into his kind care, Evelina."

"I must learn to endure loneliness," I answered sadly, about to begin to gulp from force of example, and the pressure of long hereditary influence.

I'm glad that I did not dissolve, however, before what followed happened, for in the twinkling of two bare feet I was smothered in the embrace of Henrietta, who in her rush brought either the Pup or the Kit, I can't tell which yet, along to help her enfold me.

"I'll come stay with you forever, and we don't need no men! Don't like 'em no-how!" she was exclaiming down my back, when a drawl from the doorway made us all turn in that direction.

"Why, Henrietta, my own, can it be you who utter such cruel sentiments in my absence?" and Polk Hayes lounged into the room, with the same daring listlessness that he had used in trying to hold me in his arms out on the porch the night I had said good-by to him and Glendale, four years ago.

Henrietta's chubby little body gave a wriggle of delight, and much sentiment beamed in her rugged, small face, as she answered him with enthusiasm, though not stopping to couch her reply in exactly complimentary terms.

"You don't count, Pokie," she exclaimed, as she made a good-natured face at him.

"That's what Evelina said four years ago - and she has proved it," he answered her, looking at me just exactly as if he had never left off doing it since that last dance.

"How lovely to find you in the same exuberant spirits in which I left you, Polk, dear," I exclaimed, as I got up to go and shake hands with him, as he had sunk into the most comfortable chair in the room, without troubling to bestow that attention upon me.

Some men's hearts beat with such a strong rhythm that every feminine heart which comes within hearing distance immediately catches step, and goes to waltzing. It has been four years since mine swung around against his, at that dance, but I'm glad Cousin Martha was there, and interrupted, us enough to make me drag my eyes from his, as he looked up and I looked down.

"Please help us to persuade Evelina to come and live with James and me, Polk, dear," she said, glancing at him with the deepest confidence and affection in her eyes. There is no age-limit to Polk's victims, and Cousin Martha had always adored him.

"All women do, Evelina, why not you - live with James?" he asked, and I thought I detected a mocking flicker in his big, hazel, dangerous eyes.

"If I ever need protection it will be James - and Cousin Martha I will run to for it - but I never will," I answered him, very simply, with not a trace of the defiance I was fairly flinging at him in either my voice or manner.

Paris and London and New York are nice safe places to live in, in comparison with Glendale, Tennessee, in some respects. I wonder why I hadn't been more scared than I was last night, as the train whirled me down into proximity to Polk Hayes. But then I had had four years of forgetting him stored up as a bulwark.

"But what *are* you going to do, Evelina?" Sallie again began to question, with positive alarm in her voice, and I saw that it was time for me to produce some sort of a protector then and there - or capitulate.

And I record the fact that I wanted to go home with Sallie and Cousin Martha and the babies and - and live under the

Maria Thompson Daviess

roof of the Mossback forever. All that citizenship-feeling I had got poured into me from Jane and had tried on Dickie, good old Dickie, had spilled out of me at the first encounter with Polk.

There is a great big hunt going on in this world, and women are the ones only a short lap ahead. Can we turn and make good the fight - or won't we be torn to death? It has come to this it seems: women must either be weak, and cling so close to man that she can't be struck, keep entirely out of the range of his fists and arms, - or develop biceps equal to his. Jane ought to have had me in training longer, for I'm discovering that I'm weak - of biceps.

"Are you coming - are you coming to live with us, Evelina? Are you coming? Answer!" questioned the small Henrietta, as she stood commandingly in front of me.

"Please, Evelina," came in a coax from Sallie, while the Kit crawled over and caught at my skirt as Cousin Martha raised her eyes to mine, with a gentle echo of the combined wooings.

Then suddenly into Polk's eyes flamed still another demand, that something told me I would have to answer later. I had capitulated and closed this book forever when the deliverance came.

Jasper, a little older, but as black and pompous as ever, stood in the doorway, and a portly figure, with yellow, shining face, on the step behind him.

"Why, Uncle Jasper, how did you know I was here?" I exclaimed, as I fairly ran to hold out my hand to him.

"Mas' James sont me word last night, and I woulder been here by daybreak, Missie, 'cept I had to hunt dis yere suitable woman to bring along with me. Make your 'beesence to Miss Evelina, Lucy Petunia," he commanded.

"You needn't to bother to show her anything, child," he continued calmly, "I'll learn her all she needs to know to suit us. Then, if in a week she have shown suitable ability to please us both, my word is out to marry her next Sunday night. Ain't that the understanding, Tuny?" he this time demanded.

"Yes, sir," answered the Petunia with radiant but modest hope shining from her comely yellow face.

"I've kept everything ready for you child, since Old Mas' died, and I ain't never stayed offen the place a week at a time - I was just visiting out Petunia's way when I heard you'd come, and gittin' a wife to tend to us and back to you quick was the only thing that concerned me. Now, we can all settle down comf'table, while I has Tuny knock up some dinner, a company one I hopes, if Miss Martha and the rest will stay with us." Jasper's manner is an exact copy of my Father's courtly grace, done in sepia, and my eyes misted for a second, as I reciprocated his invitation, taking acceptance for granted.

"Of course they will stay, Uncle Jasper."

"Well," remarked Sallie with a gasp, "you've gone to housekeeping in two minutes, Evelina."

"Jasper has always been a very forceful personality," said Cousin Martha. "He managed everything for your Father at the last, Evelina, and I don't know how the whole town would have been easy about the Colonel unless they had trusted Jasper."

"I like the terms on which he takes unto himself a wife,"

drawled Polk, as he lighted a cigarette without looking at me. "Good for Jasper!"

"However, it does take a 'forceful personality' to capture a 'suitable woman' in that manner," I answered with just as much unconcern, and then we both roared, while even Sallie in all her anxiety joined in.

The commanding, black old man, and the happy-faced, plump, little yellow woman, had saved one situation - and forced another, perhaps?

Jasper's home-coming dinner party was a large and successful one. Two of the dear little old Horton lady-cousins got so impatient at Cousin Martha's not bringing me back to Widegables that they came teetering over to see about it, heavily accompanied by Mrs. Hargrove, whose son had been Cousin James's best friend at the University of Virginia, and died and left her to him since I had been at college. The ponderosity of her mind was only equaled by that of her body. I must say Petunia made a hit with the dear old soul, by the seasoning of her chicken gravy.

Sallie wanted to send the children home, but Jasper wouldn't let her, and altogether we had eleven at the table.

Polk maneuvered for a seat at the head of my festive board, with a spark of the devil in his eyes, but Jasper's sense of the proprieties did not fail me, and he seated Cousin Martha in Father's chair, with great ceremony.

And as I looked down the long table, bright with all the old silver Jasper had had time to polish, gay with roses from my garden, that he had coaxed Henrietta into gathering for him, which nodded back and forth with the bubbling babies, suddenly my heart filled to the very brim with love of it all - and for mine own people.

But, just as suddenly, a vision came into my mind of the long table across the road at Widegables, with the Mossback seated at one end with only two or three of his charges stretched along the empty sides to keep him company.

I wanted him to be here with us! I wanted him badly, and I went to get him. I excused myself suddenly, telling them all just why. I didn't look at Polk, but Cousin Martha's face was lovely, as she told me to run quickly.

I found him on the front porch, smoking his pipe alone, while the two little relics, whom he had had left to dine with him, were taking their two respective naps. Our dinner was late on account of the initiation of Petunia, and he had finished before we began.

"I stole most of your family to-day," I plunged headlong into my errand, "but I want you, too, most of all."

"You've got me, even if you do prefer to keep me across the road from you," he answered, with the most solemn expression on his face, but with a crinkle of a smile in the corners of his deep eyes.

I can't remember when I didn't look with eagerness for that crinkle in his eyes, even when I was a child and he what I at that time considered a most glorious grownup individual, though he must have been the most helpless hobbledehoy that ever existed.

"You don't need another vine," I answered mutinously.

"You know I want you, but Jasper's is the privilege of looking after you," he answered calmly. "I want you to be

Maria Thompson Daviess

happy, Evelina," and I knew as I raised my eyes to his that I could consider myself settled in my own home.

"Well, then, come and have dinner number two with me," I answered with a laugh that covered a little happy sigh that rose from my heart at the look in the kind eyes bent on mine.

I felt, Jane, you would have approved of that look! It was so human to human.

He came over with me, and that was one jolly party in the old dining-room. They all stayed until almost sunset, and almost everybody in town dropped in during the afternoon to welcome me home, and ask me where I was going to live. Jasper and Petunia hovering in the background, the tea-tray out on the porch set with the silver and damask all of them knew of old, and the appearance of having been installed with the full approval of Cousin Martha and James and the rest of the family, stopped the questions on their lips, and they spent the afternoon much enlivened but slightly puzzled.

Time doesn't do much to people in a place like the Harpeth Valley, that is out of the stream of modern progress; and most of my friends seem to have just been sitting still, rocking their lives along in the greatest ease and comfort.

Still, Mamie Hall has three more kiddies, which, added to the four she had when I left, makes a slightly high, if charming, set of stair-steps. Mamie also looks decidedly worn, though pathetically sweet. Ned was with her, and as fresh as any one of the buds. Maternity often wilts women, but paternity is apt to make men bloom with the importance of it. Ned showed off the bunch as if he had produced them all, while Mamie only smiled like an angel in the background.

A slight bit of temper rose in a flush to my cheeks, as I watched Caroline Lellyett sit on the steps and feed cake to one twin and two stair-steps with as much hunger in her eyes for them as there was in theirs for the cake. Lee Greenfield is the responsible party in this case, and she has been loving him hopelessly for fifteen years. Lots of other folks wanted to marry her, but Lee has pinned her in the psychic spot and is watching her flutter.

Polk departed in the trail of Nell Kirkland's fluffy muslin skirts, smoldering dangerously, I felt. Nell has grown up into a most lovely individual, and I felt uneasy about her under Folk's ministrations. Her eyes follow him rather persistently. On the whole, I am glad Jane committed me to this woman's cause. I'll have to begin to exercise the biceps of Nell's heart - as soon as I get some strength into my own.

And after they had all gone, I sat for an hour out on the front steps of my big, empty old house, and enjoyed my own loneliness, if it could be called enjoying. I could hear the Petunia's happy giggle, answering Jasper's guttural pleasantries, out on the cabin porch behind the row of lilac bushes. I do hope that Petunia gets much and the right sort of courting during this week that Jasper has allowed her!

With the last rays of the sun, I had found time to read a long, dear letter from Richard Hall, and though I had transferred it from my pocket to my desk, while I dressed for the afternoon, its crackle was still in my mind. I wondered what it all meant, this dissatisfied longing that human beings send out across time and distance, one to and for another.

If a woman's heart were really like a great big golden chalice, full to the brim with the kind of love she is taught God wants her to have in it for all mankind, both men and women, why shouldn't she offer drafts of it to every one who is thirsty, brothers as well as sisters? I wonder how that would solve Jane's problem of emotional equality! I do love Dicky - and - and I do love Polk - with an inclination to dodge. Now, if there were enough of the right sort of love in me, I ought to be able to get them to see it, and drink it for their comforting, and have no trouble at all with them about their wanting to seize the cup, drain all the love there is in it, shut it away from the rest of the world - and then neglect it.

Yes, why can't I love Polk as I love you, Jane, and have him enjoy it? Yes, why?

I think if I had Dicky off to myself for a long time, and very gently led him up to the question of loving him hard in this new way, he might be induced to sip out of the cup just to see if he liked it - and it might be just what he craved, for the time being; but I doubt it. He would storm and bluster at the idea.

Of course the Crag would let a woman love him in any old kind of new or experimental way she wanted to, if it made her happy. He would take her cup of tenderness and drink it as if it were sacramental wine, on his knees. But he doesn't count. He has to be man to so many people that there is danger of his becoming a kind of superman. Think of the old Mossback being a progressive thing like that! I laughed out loud at the idea - but the echo was dismal.

I wonder if Sallie will marry him.

And as I sat and thought and puzzled, the moonlight got

richer and more glowing, and it wooed open the throats of the thousand little honeysuckle blossoms, clinging to the vine on the trellis, until they poured out a perfect symphony of perfume to mingle in a hallelujah from the lilacs and roses that ascended to the very stars themselves.

I had dropped my head on my arms, and let my eyes go roaming out to the dim hills that banked against the radiant sky, when somebody seated himself beside me, and a whiff of tobacco blew across my face, sweet with having joined in the honeysuckle chorus. Nobody said a word for a long time, and then I looked up and laughed into the deep, gray eyes looking tenderly down into mine. With a thrill I realized that there was one man in the world I could offer the chalice to and *trust* him to drink - moderately.

"Jamie," I said in a voice as young as it used to be when I trailed at his heels, "thank you for letting me be contrary and independent and puzzling. I have been busy adventuring with life, in queer places and with people not like - like us. Now I want a little of real living and to think - and feel. May I?"

"You may, dear," the Crag answered in a big comfortable voice, that was a benediction in itself. "I understood last night when you told me that you wanted to come home alone. I can trust Jasper with you, and I am going to sleep down at the lodge room, right across the road here, so I can hear you if you even think out loud. No one shall worry you about it any more. Now will you promise to be happy?"

I could not answer him, I was so full of a deepness of peace. I just laid my cheek against the sleeve of his queer old gray coat, to show him what I could not say.

He let me do it, and went on smoking without noticing me.

Then, after a little while, he began to tell me all about Father and his death, that had come so suddenly while he seemed as well as ever, and how he had worried about my probably not wanting to be left to him, and that he wanted me to feel independent, but to please let him do all that I would to help me, and not to feel that I was alone with nobody to love me. That he was always there, and would be forever and ever.

And he did stay so late that Jasper had to send him home!

There is such a thing as a man's being a father and mother and grown sister and brother and a college-chum and a preacher of the Gospel and a family physician to a woman - with no possibility of being her husband either. She wouldn't so drag such a man from his high estate as to think of such a worldly relation in connection with him.

I have certainly collected some phenomena in the reaction of a woman's heart this day. Did you choose me wisely for these experiments, Jane?

It takes a woman of nerve to go to housekeeping in a tinder-box, when she isn't sure she even knows what flint is when she sees it, and might strike out a spark without intending it at all.

CHAPTER IV

SWEETER WHEN TAMED?

I wonder if men ever melt suddenly into little boys, and try to squirm and run back to hide their heads in their mothers' skirts. It is an open secret that starchy, modern women often long to wilt back into droopy musk roses, that climb over gates and things, but they don't let each other. When I feel myself getting soluble, I write it out to Jane and I get a bracing cold wave of a letter in reply. The one this morning was on the subject of love, or, at least, that is what Jane would have said it was on. She wrote:

> Yes, it is gratifying to know that Mary Elizabeth is so happily engaged to the young teacher who has been in her work with her. She writes that she was encouraged by our resolution, at last to be her best self while in his presence as she had not had the courage to do last year. You see, Evelina? And also, you are right in your conclusion that there is not enough abstract love in this world of brotherhood and sisterhood; that the doctrine of divine love calls us to give more and more of it. We cannot give too much! But also, considerations for the advancement of the world call for experiments by the more illumined women along more definite and concrete lines. How old is this Mr. Hayes, on whom you have chosen to note the reactions of sisterly affection? Are you sure

Maria Thompson Daviess

that he is not a fit subject for your consideration in the matter of a choice for a mate?

Remember to be as frank in your expressions of regard for him as he is in his of regard for you. That is the crux of the whole matter. Be frank, be courageous! Let a man look freely into your heart, and thus encouraged he will open his to you. Then you will both have an opportunity to judge each other with reference to a life-long union. It is the only way; and remember what rests on you in this matter. The destinies of many women are involved.

*   *   *   *   *

I don't say this in a spirit of levity, but I do wish Polk Hayes and Jane Mathers were out on the front steps in the moonlight, after a good supper that has made him comfortable, Jane to be attired in something soft that would float against his arm, whether she wanted it to or not! I believe it would be good for Jane, and make things easier for me. Be frank with Polk as to how much he asphyxiates me? I know better than to blow out the gas like that! No, Jane!

But what is a woman going to do when she is young and hearty and husky, with the blood running through her veins at a two-forty rate, when her orchard is in bloom, the mocking-birds are singing the night through, and she is not really in love with anybody? The loneliness does fill her heart full of the solution of love, and she has got to pour off some of it into somebody's life. There is plenty of me to be both abstract and concrete, at the same time, and I thought of Uncle Peter.

Uncle Peter Is the most explosive and crusty person that ever happened in Glendale, and it takes all of Aunt

Augusta's energy, common-sense and force of character to keep him and the two chips he carries on his shoulders, as a defiance to the world in general, from being in a constant state of combustion. He has been ostensibly the Mayor of Glendale for twenty-five years, and Aunt Augusta has done the work of the office very well indeed, while he has blown up things in general with great energy. He couldn't draw a long breath without her, but of course he doesn't realize it. He thinks he is in a constant feud with her and her sex. His ideas on the woman question are so terrific that I have always run from them, but I concluded that it would be a good thing for me to liquefy some of my vague humanitarianism, and help Aunt Augusta with him, while she wrestles with the City Council on the water question. Anyway, I have always had a guarded fondness for the old chap.

I chose a time when I knew Aunt Augusta had to be busy with his report of the disastrous concrete paving trade the whole town had been sold out on, and I lay in wait to capture him and the chips. This morning I waited behind the old purple lilac at the gate, which immediately got into the game by sweeping its purple-plumed arms all around me, so that not a tag of my dimity alarmed him as he came slowly down the street.

"Uncle Peter," I said, as I stepped out in front of him suddenly, "please, Uncle Peter, won't you come in and talk to me?"

"Hey? Evelina?"

"Yes, Uncle Peter, it's Evelina," and I hesitated with terror at the snap in his dear old eyes, back under their white brows. Then I let my eyes uncover my heart full of the elixir I had prepared for him, and offered him as much as he could drink.

"I'm lonely," I said, with a little catch in my voice.

"Lonely - hey?" he grumbled, but his feet hesitated opposite my gate.

In about two and a half minutes I had him seated in a cushioned rocker on the south side of the porch. Jasper had given us both a mint julep, and Uncle Peter was much Jess thirsty than he had been for a long time. Aunt Augusta is as temperate in all things as a steel ramrod.

"You see, Uncle Peter, I needed you so that I just had to kidnap you," I said to him, as he wiped his lips with a pocket-handkerchief, as stiffly starched as was his wife herself.

"Why didn't you go over and live in James's hennery - live with James - hey?" he snapped, with the precision of a pistol cap.

To be just, I suppose Aunt Augusta's adamant disposition accounts, to some extent, for Uncle Peter's explosive way of thinking and speaking. A husband would have to knock Aunt Augusta's nature down to make any impression whatever on it. Uncle Peter always has the air of firing an idea and then ducking his head to avoid the return shot.

"His house is so full, and I need a lot of space to carry on my work," I answered him, with the words I have used so often in the last two weeks that they start to come when the Petunia asks me if I want waffles or batter-cakes for supper.

"Well, Sallie Carruthers will get him, and then there'll be a dozen more to run the measure over - children - hey? All girls! A woman like Sallie would not be content with producing less than a dozen of her kind - hey?"

His chuckle was so contagious that I couldn't help but join him, though I didn't like it so very much. But why shouldn't I? Sallie is such a gorgeous woman that a dozen of her in the next generation will be of value to the State. Still, I didn't like it. I didn't enjoy thinking of Cousin James as so serving his country.

"Carruthers left her to James - he'll have to take care of her. Henry turned toes in good time. Piled rotten old business and big family on to James's shoulders, and then died - good time - hey? Get a woman on your hands, only thing to do is to marry or kill her. Poor James - hey?" He peered at me with a twinkle in his eyes that demanded assent from me.

"Why, Uncle Peter, I don't know that Sallie has any such idea. She grieves dreadfully over Mr. Carruthers, and I don't believe she would think of marrying again," I answered, trying to put enough warmth in my defense to convince myself.

"Most women are nothing but gourd-vines, grow all over a corn-stalk, kill it, produce gourds until it frosts, and begin all over again in the next generation. James has to do the hoeing around Sallie's roots, and feed her. Might as well marry her - hey?"

"Does - does Cousin James have to support Sallie and the children, Uncle Peter?" I asked, coming with reluctance down to the rock-bed of the discussion.

"Thinks he does, and it serves him right - serves him right for starting out to run a widow-ranch in the first place; it's like making a collection of old shoes. He let Henry Carruthers persuade him to mortgage everything and buy land on the river for the car-shops of the new railroad, which just fooled the town out of a hundred thousand dollars, and is going by on the other side of the river with the shops up at Bolivar. If James didn't get all the lawing in Alton County they would all starve to death - which would be hard on the constitution of old lady Hargrove, and her two hundred-weight."

"Oh, has Cousin James really lost all of his fortune?" I asked, and I was surprised at the amount of sympathetic dismay that rose in me at the information.

"Everything but what he carries around under that old gray hat of his - not so bad a fortune, at that! - hey?"

I feel I am going to love Uncle Peter for the way he disdainfully admires Cousin James.

"And - and all of his - his guests are really dependent on him?" I asked again, as the stupendous fact filtered into my mind.

"All the flock, all the flock," answered Uncle Peter, with what seemed, under the circumstances, a heartless chuckle. "They each one have little dabs of property, about as big as a handful of chicken feed, and as they have each one given it all to James to manage, they expect an income in return - and get it - all they ask for. A lot of useless old live stock - all but Sallie, and she's worse - worse, hey?"

I agreed with his question - but I didn't say so.

"Glad your money is safe in Public Town Bonds and City Securities, Evelina. If James could, he might lose it, and you'd have to move over. It would then be nip and tuck between you and Sallie which got James - nip and tuck - hey?"

"Oh, Uncle Peter!" I exclaimed with positive horror that was flavored with a large dash of indignation.

"Well, yes, a race between a widow and a girl for a man is about like one between a young duck and a spring chicken, across a mill-pond - girl and chicken lose - hey? But let Sallie have him, since you don't need him. I've got to go home and listen to Augusta talk about my business, that she knows nothing in the world about, or I won't be ready for town meeting this afternoon. Women are all fools, - hey?"

"Will you come again, Uncle Peter?" I asked eagerly. I had set out to offer Uncle Peter a cup of niecely affection, and I had got a good, stiff bracer to arouse me in return.

"I will, whenever I can escape Augusta," he answered, and there was such a kindly crackle in his voice that I felt that he had wanted and needed what I had offered him. "I'll drop in often and analyze the annals of the town with you. Glad to have you home, child, good young blood to stir me up - hey?"

And as I sat and watched the Mayor go saunteringly down the street, with his crustiness carried like a child on his shoulder, which it delighted him to have knocked off, so that he could philosophize in the restoring of it to its position, suddenly a realization of the relation of Glendale to the world in general was forced upon me - and I quailed.

Glendale is like a dozen other small towns in the Harpeth Valley; they are all drowsy princesses who have just waked up enough to be wondering what did it. The tentative kiss has not yet disclosed the presence of the Prince of Revolution, and they are likely to doze for another century or two. I think I had better go back into the wide world and let them sleep on. One live member is likely to irritate the repose of the whole body.

Their faint stirrings of progress are pathetic.

They have an electric plant, but, as I have noted before, the lights therefrom show a strong trace of their pine-knot heredity, and go out on all important occasions, whether of festivity or tragedy. Kerosene lamps have to be kept filled and cleaned if a baby or a revival or a lawn festival is expected.

They have a lovely, wide concrete pavement in front of six of the stores around the public square, but no two stretches of the improvement join each other, and it makes a shopping progression around the town somewhat dangerous, on account of the sudden change of grade of the sidewalk, about every sixty feet. Aunt Augusta wanted Uncle Peter to introduce a bill in the City Council forcing all of the property owners on the Square to put down the pavement in front of their houses, at small payments per annum, the town assuming the contract at six per cent. Uncle Peter refused, because he said that he felt a smooth walk around the Square would call out what he called "a dimity parade" every afternoon.

They have a water system that is supplied by so much mud from the river that it often happens that the town has to go unwashed for a week, while the pipes are cleaned out. There is a wonderful spring that could be used, with a pump to supply the town, Aunt Augusta says.

The City Council tied up the town for a hundred thousand dollars' subscription to the new railroad, and failed to tie the shops down in the contract. They are to be built in Bolivar. A great many of the rich men have lost a lot of money thereby, Cousin James the most of all, and everybody is sitting up in bed blinking.

There are still worse things happening in the emotional realm of Glendale.

Lee Greenfield has been in the state of going to ask Caroline Lellyett to marry him for fifteen years, and has never done it. Caroline has been beautiful all her life, but she is getting so thin and faded at thirty that she is a tragedy. Lee goes to see her twice a week, and on Sunday afternoon takes her out in his new and rakish runabout, that is as modern as his behavior is obsolete. Caroline knows no better, and stands it with sublime patience and lack of character. That is a situation I won't be able to keep my hands off of much longer.

Ned Hall's wife has seven children with the oldest one not twelve, and she looks fifty. Ned goes to all the dances at the Glendale Hotel dining-room and looks thirty. He dresses beautifully and Nell and all the girls like to dance with him. Just ordinary torture wouldn't do for him.

Polk Hayes wouldn't be allowed to run loose in London society.

Sallie Carruthers is a great big husky woman, with three children that she is responsible for having had. She and her family must consume tons of green groceries every month and a perfectly innocent man pays for them.

Mrs. Dodd, the carpenter-and-contractor's wife is a Boston woman who came down here - Before I could write all about that Boston girl so that Jane could understand perfectly the situation Polk came around from the side street and seated himself on the railing of the porch so near the arm of my chair that I couldn't rock without inconveniencing him.

Maria Thompson Daviess

I am glad he found me in the mood I was in and I am glad to record the strong-minded - it came near being the strong-armed - contest in which we indulged.

"Me for a woman that has a lot of spirit - she is so much sweeter when tamed, Evelina," was one of the gentle remarks with which he precipitated the riot. "I think it has been spunkily fascinating of you to come and live by yourself in this old barn. It keeps me awake nights just to think of you over here - alone. How long is the torture to go on?"

Jane, I tried, but if I had frankly and courageously shown Polk Hayes what was in my heart for him at that moment, I couldn't have answered for the results.

From the time I was eighteen until I was twenty the same sort of assault and battery had been handed out to me from him. He had beaten me with his love. He didn't want me - he doesn't want any woman except so long as he is uncertain that he can get her. Just because I had been firm with him when even a child and denied him, he has been merciless. And now that I am a woman and armed for the combat, it will be to the death.

Shall I double and take refuge in a labyrinth of subterfuge or turn and fight? So I temporized to-day.

"It is lonely - but not quite 'torture' to me, with the family so close, across the street," I answered him, and I went on whipping the lace on a piece of fluff I am making, to discipline myself because I loathe a needle so. "Please don't you worry over me, dear." I raised my eyes to his and I tried the common citizenship look. It must have carried a little way for he flushed, the first time I ever saw him do it, and his hand with the cigarette in it shook.

"Evelina, are you real or a - farce?" he asked, after a few minutes of peace.

"I'm trying to be real, Polk," I answered, and this time I raised my eyes with perfect frankness. "If you could define a real woman, Polk, in what terms would you express her?" I asked him straight out from the shoulder.

"Hell fire and a hallelujah chorus, if she's beautiful," he answered me promptly.

I laughed. I thought it was best under the circumstances.

"I'll tell you, Evelina," he continued, stealthily. "A man just can't generalize the creatures. Apparently they are craving nothing so much as emotional excitement and when you offer it to them they want to go to house-keeping with it. Love is a business with them and not an art."

"Would you like to try a genuine friendship with one. Polk?" I asked, and again struck from the shoulder - with my eyes.

"Help! Not if you mean yourself, beautiful," he answered promptly and with fervor. "I wouldn't trust myself with you one minute off-guard like that."

"You could safely."

"But I won't!"

"Will you try?"

"No!"

"Will you go over and sit in that chair while I tell you

something calmly, quietly, and seriously? It'll give you a new sensation and maybe it will be good for you." I looked him straight in the face and the battle of our eyes was something terrific. I had made up my mind to have it out with him then and there. There was nothing else to do. I would be frank and courageous and true to my vow - and accept the consequences.

He slid along the railing of the porch and down into the chair in almost a daze of bewilderment.

"Polk," I began, concealing a gulp of terror, "I love you more than I can possibly - "

"Say, Polk, I let the Pup git hung by her apron to the wheel of your car out in the road and her head is dangersome kinder upside down. It might run away. Can you come and git her loose for me?"

Henrietta's calmness under dire circumstances was a lesson to both Polk and me, for with two gasps that sounded as one we both raced across the porch, down the path and out to the road where Folk's Hupp runabout stood by the worn old stone post that had tethered the horses of the wooers of many generations of the maids of my house.

But, prompt as our response to Henrietta's demand for rescue had been, Cousin James was there before us. He stood in the middle of the dusty road with the tousled mite in his arms, soothing her frightened sobs against his cheek with the dearest tenderness and patting Sallie on the back with the same comforting.

"Oh, Henrietta, how could you nearly kill your little sister like this?" Sallie sobbed. "Please say something positive to her, James!"

"Henrietta," began Cousin James with a suspicion of embarrassment at Polk's and my presence at the domestic scene. Polk choked a chuckle and I could have murdered him.

"Wait a minute," said Henrietta, in her most commanding voice. "Sallie, didn't you ask me to take that Pup from Aunt Dilsie, 'cause of the phthisic, and keep her quiet while the Kit got a nap, and didn't I ask you if it would be all right if I got her back whole and clean?"

"Yes, Henrietta, but you -"

"Ain't she whole all over and clean?"

"Yes, but - "

"Couldn't nobody do any better than that with one of them twins. I won't try. If I have to 'muse her it has to be in my own way." And with her head in the air the Bunch marched up the walk to the house.

At this Polk shouted and the rest of us laughed.

"Polk, please don't encourage Henrietta in the way she treats me and her little sisters," Sallie begged between her laughs and her half-swallowed sobs. "I need my friends' help with my children, not to have them make it hard for me. Henrietta is devoted to you and you could influence her so for the best. Please try to help me make a real woman out of her and not some sort of a terrible - terrible suffragette."

Sallie is the most perfectly lovely woman I almost ever saw. She has great violet eyes with black lashes that beg you for a piece of your heart, and her mouth is as sweet as a blush rose with cheeks that almost match it in rosiness.

Maria Thompson Daviess

She and the babies always remind me of a cluster rose and roses, flower and buds, and I don't see why every man that sees her is not mad about her. They all used to be before she married, and I suppose they will be again as soon as the crepe gets entirely worn off her clothes. As she stood with the bubbly baby in her arms and looked up at Polk I couldn't see how he could take it calmly.

"Sallie," he answered seriously, with a glint in his eyes over at me, "if you'll give me a few days longer, I will then have found out by experience what a real woman is and I'll begin on Henrietta for you accordingly."

"Don't be too hard on the kiddie," Cousin James answered him with the crinkle in the corner of his eyes that might have been called shrewd in eyes less beautifully calm. "Let's trust a lot to Henrietta's powers of observation of her mother and - her neighbors." He smiled suddenly, with his whole face, over both Sallie and me, and went on down the street in a way that made me sure he was forgetting all about all of us before he reached the corner of the street.

"Isn't that old mossback a treat for the sight of gods and men?" asked Polk with a laugh as we all stood watching the old gray coat-tails flapping in the warm breeze that was rollicking across the valley.

"I don't know what I would do without him," said Sadie softly, with tears suddenly misting the violets in her eyes as she turned away from us with the baby in her arms and went slowly up the front walk of Widegables.

"Please come stay with me a little while, Evelina," she pleaded back over her shoulder. "I feel faint."

I hesitated, for, as we were on my side of the Road, Polk

was still my guest.

"Go on with Sallie, sweetie," he answered my hesitating.
"I don't want the snapped-off fraction of a declaration like
you were about to offer me. I can bide my time - and get
my own." With which he turned and got into his car as I
went across the street.

Jane, I feel encouraged. I have done well to-day to get
half way through my declaration of independence -
though he doesn't think that is what it is going to be - to
Polk. If I can just tell him how much I love him, before he
makes love to me we can get on such a sensible footing
with each other. I'll command the situation then.

But suppose I do get Polk calmed down to a nice friendship after old Plato's recipe, what if I want to marry him?

Do I want to marry a friend?

Yes, I do!

No - no!

CHAPTER V

DEEPER THAN SHOULDERS AND RIBS

There are many fundamental differences between men and women which strike deeper than breadth of shoulders and number of ribs on the right side.

Men deliberately unearth matters of importance and women stumble on the same things in the dark. It is then a question of the individual as to the complications that result. One thing can be always counted on. A woman likes to tangle life into a large mass and then straighten out the threads at her leisure - and the man's leisure too.

Glendale affairs interest me more every day.

This has been a remarkable afternoon and I wish Jane had been in Glendale to witness it.

"Say, Evelina, all the folks over at our house have gone crazy, and I wish you would come over and help Cousin James with 'em," Henrietta demanded, as I sat on my side porch, calmly hemming a ruffle on a dress for the Kitten. Everybody sews for the twins and, as much as I hate it, I can't help doing it.

"Why, Henrietta, what is the matter?" I demanded, as I hurried down the front walk and across the road at her bare little heels. By the time I got to the front gate I could hear sounds of lamentation.

"A railroad train wants to run right through the middle of all their dead people and Sallie started the crying. Dead's dead, and if Cousin James wants 'em run over. I wants 'em run over too." She answered over her shoulder as we hurried through the wide front hall.

And a scene that beggars description met my eyes, as I stood in the living-room door. I hope this account I am going to try and write will get petrified by some kind of new element they will suddenly discover some day and the manuscript be dug up from the ruins of Glendale to interest the natives of the Argon age about 2800 A. D.

Sallie sat in the large armchair in the middle of the room weeping in the slow, regular way a woman has of starting out with tears, when she means to let them flow for hours, maybe days, and there were just five echoes to her grief, all done in different keys and characters.

Cousin Martha knelt beside the chair and held Sallie's head on her ample bosom, but I must say that the expression on her face was one of bewilderment, as well as of grief.

The three little Horton cousins sat close together in the middle of the old hair-cloth sofa by the window and were weeping as modestly and helplessly as they did everything else in life, while Mrs. Hargrove, in her chair under her son's portrait, was just plainly out and out howling.

And on the hearth-rug, before the tiny fire of oak chips that the old ladies liked to keep burning all summer, stood the master of the house and, for once in my life, I have seen the personification of masculine helplessness. He

Maria Thompson Daviess

was a tragedy and I flew straight to him with arms wide open, which clasped both his shoulders as I gave him a good shake to arouse him from his paralyzation.

"What's the matter?" I demanded, with the second shake.

"I'm a brute, Evelina," he answered, and a sudden discouragement lined every feature of his beautiful biblical face. I couldn't stand that and I hugged him tight to my breast for an instant and then administered another earthquake shake.

"Tell me exactly what has happened," I demanded, looking straight into his tragic eyes and letting my hands slip from his shoulders down his arms until they held both of his hands tight and warm in mine.

Jane, I was glad that I had offered the cup of my eyes to him full of this curious inter-sex elixir of life that you have induced me to seek so blindly, for he responded to the dose immediately and the color came back into his face as he answered me just as sensibly as he would another man.

"The men who are surveying the new railroad from Cincinnati to the Gulf have laid their experimental lines across the corner of Greenwood Cemetery and they say it will have to run that way or go across the river and parallel the lines of the other road. If they come on this side of the river they will force the other road to come across, too, and in that case we will get the shops. It just happens that such a line will make necessary the removal of - of poor Henry's remains to another lot. Sallie's is the only lot in the cemetery that is that high on the bluff. Henry didn't like the situation when he bought it himself, and I thought that, as there is another lot right next to her mother's for sale, she would not - but, of course, I was brutal to mention it to her. I hope you will find it in your heart to forgive me, Sallie." And as he spoke he extracted himself from me and walked over and laid his hand on Sallie's head.

"It was such a shock to her - poor Henry," sobbed little Cousin Jasmine, and the other two little sisters sniffed in chorus.

"To have railroad trains running by Greenwood at all will be disturbing to the peace of the dead," snorted Mrs. Hargrove. "We need no railroad in Glendale. We have never had one, and that is my last word - no!"

"Four miles to the railroad station across the river is just a pleasant drive in good weather," said Cousin Martha, plaintively, as she cuddled Sallie's sobs more comfortably down on her shoulder.

"I feel that Henry would doubt my faithfulness to his memory, if I consented to such a desecration," came in smothered tones from the pillowing shoulder.

And not one of all those six women had stopped to think for one minute that the minor fact of the disturbing of the ashes of Henry Carruthers would be followed by the major one of the restoration of the widow's fortune and the lifting of a huge financial burden off the strong shoulders they were all separately and collectively leaning upon.

I exploded, but I am glad I drew the Crag out on the porch and did it to him alone.

"Evelina, you are refreshing if strenuous," he laughed, after I had spent five minutes in stating my opinions of women in general and a few in particular. "But I ought not to have hurt Sallie by telling her about the lines until they are a certainty. It is so far only a possibility. They may go across the river anyway."

"And as for seeing Sallie swaddled in your consideration, and fed yourself as a sacrifice from a spoon, I am tired of it," I flamed up again. "It's not good for her. Feed and clothe her and her progeny, - men in general have brought just such burdens as that upon you in particular by their attitude towards us, - but do let her begin to exert just a small area of her brain on the subject of the survival of the fit to live. You don't swaddle or feed me!"

"Eve," he said, softly under his breath as his wonderful gentle eyes sank down way below the indignation and explosiveness to the quiet pool that lies at the very bottom of my heart.

Nobody ever found it before and I didn't know it was there myself, but I felt as if it were being drained up into Heaven.

"Eve!" He said again, and it is a wonder that I didn't answer:

"Adam!"

I don't know just what would have happened if Uncle Peter hadn't broken in on the interview with his crustiest chips on both shoulders and so much excitement bottled up that he had to let it fly like a double reporter.

"Dodson is down at the Hotel looking for you, James," he began as he hurried up the steps. "Big scheme this - got him in a corner if the C. & G. comes along this side of Old Harpeth - make him squeal - hey?"

"Who's Dodson?" I asked with the greatest excitement. I was for the first time getting a whiff of the schemes of the masculine mighty, but I was squelched promptly by Uncle Peter.

"We've no time for questions, Evelina, now - go back to your tatting - hey?" He answered me as he began to buttonhole the Crag and lead him down the steps.

"Dodson is the man who is laying down and contracting for the line across the river, Evelina," answered Cousin James without taking any notice whatever of Uncle Peter's squelching of me. "If this other line can just be secured he will have to come to our terms - and the situation will be saved." As he spoke he took my hand in his and led me at his side, down the front walk to the gate, talking as he went, for Uncle Peter was chuckling on ahead like a steam tug in a hurry.

"And the shades of Henry will again assume the maintenance of his family," I hazarded with lack of respect of the dead, impudence to Cousin James about his own affairs, and unkindness by implication to Sallie, who loves me better than almost anybody in the world does. And I got my just punishment by seeing a lovely look of tender concern rise in Cousin James's eyes as he stopped short in the middle of the walk.

"I want to go back a minute to speak to Sallie before I go on down town," he said, quickly, and before Uncle Peter's remonstrances had exploded, he had taken the steps two at a bound and disappeared in the front door.

"Sooner he marries that lazy lollypop the better," fumed Uncle Peter, as he waited at the gate. "The way for a man to quench his thirst for woman-sweets is to marry a pot of honey like that, and then come right on back to the bread and butter game. Here's a letter Jasper gave me to bring along for you from town. Go on and read it and do not disturb the workings of my brain while I wait for James - workings of a great brain - hey?"

I took the letter and hurried across the street because I wanted anyway to get to some place by myself and think. There was no earthly reason for it but I felt like an animal that has been hurt and wants to go off and lick its wounds. A womanly woman that lives a lovely appealing life right in a man's own home has a perfect right to gain his love, especially if she is beautifully unconscious of her appeal. Besides, why should a man want to take an independent, explosive, impudent firebrand with all sorts of dreadful plots in her mind to his heart? He wouldn't and doesn't!

There is no better sedative for a woman's disturbed and wounded emotions than a little stiff brain work. Richard's letter braced my viny drooping of mind at once and from thinking into the Crag's affairs of sentiment, I turned with masculine vigor to begin to mix into his affairs of finance. However, I wish that the first big business letter I ever got in my life hadn't had to have a strain of love interest running through it! Still Dickie is a trump card in the man pack.

It seems that as his father is one of the most influential directors and largest stockholders in this new branch of the Cincinnati and Gulf railroad he has got the commission for making the plans for all the stations along the road, and he wants to give me the commission for drawing all the gardens for all the station-yards. It will be tremendous for both of us so young in life, and I never dared hope for such a thing. I had only hoped to get a few private gardens of some of my friends to laze and pose over, but this is startling. My mind is beginning to work on in terms of hedges and fountains already and Dickie may be coming South any minute.

And besides the hedges and gravel paths I have a feeling that Dickie's father and the Crag and Sallie's girl-babies are fomenting around in my mind getting ready to pop the cork of an idea soon. The combination feels like some kind of a hunch - I sat still for a long time and let it seethe, while I took stock of the situation.

There is a strange, mysterious kind of peace that begins to creep across the Harpeth Valley, just as soon as the sun sinks low enough to throw the red glow over the head of Old Harpeth. I suppose it happens in other hill-rimmed valleys in other parts of the Universe, but it does seem as if God himself is looking down to brood over us, and that the valley is the hollow of His hand into which he is gathering us to rest in the darkness of His night. I felt buffeted and in need of Him as I sank down under the rose-vine over the porch and looked out across my garden to the blue and rose hills beyond.

I have been in Glendale a whole month now, and I can't see that my influence has revolutionized the town as yet. I don't seem to be of half the importance that I thought I was going to be. I have tried, and I have offered that bucket of love that I thought up to everybody, but whether they have drunk of it to profit I am sure I can't say. In fact, my loneliness has liquefied my gaseous affection into what almost looks like officiousness.

Still, I know Uncle Peter is happier than he ever was before, because he has got me to come to as a refuge from Aunt Augusta, a confidante for his views of life that he is not allowed to express at home, and also the certainty of one of Jasper's juleps.

Sallie has grown so dependent on me that my shoulders

Maria Thompson Daviess

are assuming a masculine squareness to support her weight. I am understudying Cousin James to such an extent over at Widegables that I feel like the heir to his house. Cousin Martha sends for me when the chimney smokes and the cows get sick. I have twice changed five dollars for little Cousin Jasmine, and sternly told the man from out on their farm on Providence Road that he must not root up the lavender bushes to plant turnip-greens in their places. I afterwards rented the patch from him to grow the lavender because he said he couldn't lose the price that the greens would bring him "for crotchets."

Mrs. Hargrove has given me her will to keep for her, and the sealed instructions for her burial. I hope when the time comes the two behests will strike a balance, but I doubt it.

Her ideas of a proper funeral seem to coincide with those of Queen Victoria, whom she has admired through life and mourns sincerely.

Henrietta has not been heard to indulge in profane language since I had a long talk with her last week out in the garden, that ended in stubby tears and the gift of a very lovely locket which I impressed upon her was as chaste in design as I wished her speech to become.

The twins have been provided with several very lovely pieces of wearing apparel from my rapidly skill-acquiring needle. That's on the credit side of my balance. But that is *all* - and it doesn't sound revolutionary, does it, Jane?

Petunia married Jasper according to his word of promise, and I have taught her to cook about five French dishes that he couldn't concoct to save his life, and which help her to keep him in his place. His pomposity grows daily but he eyes me with suspicion when he sees me in secret conclave with Petunia.

"We needs a man around this place," I heard him mutter the other day as I left the kitchen.

I wonder!

The garden has been weeded, replanted, trained, clipped and garnished, and my arms are as husky and strong as a boy's and my nose badly sunburned from my strenuosity with hoe and trimming scissors.

All of which I have done and done well. But when I think of all those five girls that are waiting for me to solve the emotional formula by which they can work out and establish the fact that man equals woman, I get weak in the knees.

Jane's letters are just prods.

* * * * *

Your highly cultivated artistic nature ought to be a very beautiful revelation to the spiritual character of the young Methodist divine you wrote me of in your last letter. Encourage him in every way with affectionate interest in his work, especially in the Epworth League on his country circuit. I am enclosing fifty dollars' subscription to the work and I hope you will give as much You have not mentioned Mr. Hayes for several letters. I fear you are prejudiced against him. Seek to know and weigh his character before you judge him as unfit for your love.

* * * * *

The highly spiritual Mr. Haley glared at Polk for an hour out here on my porch, when he interrupted us in one of our Epworth League talks, in such an unspiritual manner that Polk said he felt as if he had been introduced to the

Apostle Paul while he was still Saul of Tarsus. I had to pet the Dominie decorously for a week before he regained his benign manner. Of course, however, it was trying to even a highly spiritual nature like his to have Polk insist on pinning a rose in my hair right before his eyes.

About Polk I feel that I am in the midst of one of those great calm, oily stretches of ocean that a ship is rocked gently in for a few hours before the storm tosses it first to Heaven and then to hell. He is so psychic, and in a way attuned to me, that he partly understands my purpose in declaring my love for him to put him at a disadvantage in his love-making to me, and he hasn't let me do it yet, while his tacit suit goes on. It is a drawn battle between us and is going to be fought to the death. In the meantime Nell -

And while I was on the porch sitting with Richard Hall's letter in my hand, still unread, Nell herself came down the front walk and sat down beside me.

"Why, I thought you had gone fishing with Polk," I said as I cuddled her up to me a second. She laid her head on my shoulder and heaved such a sigh that it shook us both.

"I didn't quite like to go with him alone and Henrietta wouldn't go because a bee had stung the red-headed twin, and she wanted to stay to scold Sallie," she answered with both hesitation and depression in her voice.

"Polk is - is strenuous for a whole day's companionship," I answered, experimentally, for I saw the time had come to exercise some of the biceps in Nell's femininity in preparation for just what I knew she was to get from Polk. My heart ached for what I knew she was suffering. I had had exactly those growing pains for months following that experience with him on the front porch after the dance four years ago. And I had had change of scene and occupation to help.

"I don't understand him at all," faltered Nell, and she raised her eyes as she bared her wound to me.

"Nell," I said with trepidation, as I began on this my first disciple, "you aren't a bit ashamed or embarrassed or humiliated in showing me that you love me, are you?"

"You know I've adored you ever since I could toddle at your heels, Evelina," she answered, and the love-message her great brown eyes flashed into mine was as sweet as anything that ever happened to me.

"Then, why should you wonder and suffer and restrain and be humiliated at your love for Polk?" I asked, firing point blank at all of Nell's traditions. "Why not tell him about it and ask him if he loves you?"

The shot landed with such force that Nell gasped, but answered as straight out from the shoulder as I had aimed.

"I would rather die than have Polk Hayes know how he - he affects me," she answered with her head held high.

"Then, what you feel for him is not worthy love, but something entirely unworthy," I answered loftily, with a very poor imitation of Jane's impressiveness of speech.

"I know it," she faltered into my shoulder, "if it were Mr. James Hardin I loved, I wouldn't mind anybody's knowing it, but something must be wrong with Polk or me or the way I feel. What is it?"

For a moment I got so stiff all over that Nell raised her head from my shoulder in surprise. Do all women feel about the Crag as I do?

"I don't know," I answered weakly.

And I don't know! Oh, Jane, your simple experiment proposition is about to become compound quadratics.

Then I got a still further surprise.

"I wouldn't in the least mind telling Mr. James how I like him - if you think it is all right," Nell mused, looking pensively at the first pale star that was rising over Old Harpeth. "I would enjoy it, because I have always adored him, and it would be so interesting to see what he'd say."

"Nell," I said suddenly with determination, "do it! Tell any man you like how much you like him - and see what happens."

"I feel as if - as if" - Nell faltered and I don't blame her; I wouldn't have said as much to her - "I feel that to tell Mr. James I love *him* would ease the pain, the - pain - that I feel about Polk. It would be so interesting to tell a man a thing like that."

"Do it!" I gasped, and went foot in the class in romantics.

If any jungle explorer thinks he has mapped and charted a woman's heart he had better pack up his instruments of warfare and recorders and come down to Glendale, Tennessee.

Nell and I must have talked further along the same lines, but I don't remember what we said. I have recorded the high lights on the conversation, but long after I lost her I kept my whirlwind feeling of amazement. It was like trying to balance calmly on the lid of the tinder-box when you didn't know whether or not you had touched off the fuse.

Has honeysuckle-garbed Old Harpeth been seeing things like this go on for centuries and not interrupted? I think I would have been sitting there questioning him until now, if Lee and Caroline hadn't stopped at the gate and called to me.

I think Lee was giving Caroline this stroll home from the post-office in the twilight as an extra treat in her week's allowance of him, and she was so soft and glowing and sweet and pale that I wonder the Cherokee roses on my hedge didn't droop their heads with humility before her.

"What's a lovely lady doing sitting all by herself in the gloaming?" Lee asked in his rich, warm voice.

I hate him!

"Come take a walk with us, Evelina, dear," Caroline begged softly, though I knew what it would mean to her if I should intrude on this precious hour with her near-lover.

Please, God - if I seem to be calling You into a profane situation I can't help it; I must have help! - show me some way to assist Caroline to make Lee into a real man and then get him for herself. She must have him and he needs her. And show me a way quick! Amen!

Jane, I hope you will be able to pick the data out of this jumble, but I doubt it. Anyway I'm grateful for the lock and key on this book.

As I stood at the gate and watched Lee and Caroline saunter down the moon-flecked street a mocking bird in the tallest of the oak twins that are my roof shelter called

Maria Thompson Daviess

wooingly from one of the top boughs and got his answer from about the same place on the same limb.

If a woman starts out to be a trained nurse to an epidemic of love-making, she is in great danger of doing something foolish her own self. I am even glad it is prayer-meeting night for Mr. Haley; he is safe in performing his rituals. He might misunderstand this mood.

I wonder if I ever was really over in sunny France being wooed and happy!

Of course, I decided the first night I was here that, as circumstances over which I had no control had decreed that Cousin James should stand in the position of enforced protector to me, decent, communistic femino-masculine honor demands that I refrain from any manoeuvers in his direction to attract his thoughts and attention to the feminine me. I can only meet him on the ordinary grounds of fellowship. And I suppose the glad-to-see him coming up the street was of the neuter gender, but it was very interesting.

"What did Dodson have to say - is he coming across?" I demanded of him before he got quite to my gate.

"Not if he can help it," he answered as he came close and leaned against one of the tall stone posts, so that his grandly shaped head with its ante-bellum squirls of hair was silhouetted against the white-starred wistaria vine in a way that made me frantic for several buckets of mono-chrome water-colors and a couple of brushes as big as those used for white-washing. In about ten great splotches I could have done a masterpiece of him that would have drawn artistic fits from the public of gay Paris. I never see him that I don't long for a box of pastels or get the ghost of the odor of oil-paint in my nose.

"The whole thing will be settled in a month," he continued, with a sigh that had a hint of depression in it and an astral shape of Sallie manifested itself hanging on his shoulder. However, I controlled myself and listened to him. "There is to be a meeting of the directors of both roads over in Bolivar in a few weeks and they are to come to some understanding. The line across the river is unquestionably the cheapest and best grade and there is no chance of getting them to run along our bluff - unless we can show them some advantage in doing so, and I can't see what that will be."

"What makes it of advantage for a railroad to run through any given point in a rural community like this, Cousin James?" I asked, with a glow of intellect mounting to my head, the like of which I hadn't felt since I delivered my Junior thesis in Political Economy with Jane looking on, consumed with pride.

"Towns that have good stock or grain districts around them with good roads for hauling do what is called 'feeding' a railroad," he answered. "Bolivar can feed both roads with the whole of the Harpeth Valley on that side of the river. They'll get the roads, I'm thinking. Poor old Glendale!"

"Isn't there anything to feed the monsters this side of the river?" I demanded, indignant at the barrenness of the south side of the valley of Old Harpeth.

"Very little unless it's the scenery along the bluff," he replied, with the depression sounding still more clearly in his voice and his shoulders drooped against the unsympathetic old stone post in a way that sent a pang to my heart.

"Jamie, is all you've got tied up in the venture?" I asked

Maria Thompson Daviess

softly, using the name that a very small I had given him in a long ago when the world was young and not full of problems.

"That's not the worst, Evelina," he answered in a voice that was positively haggard. "But what belongs to the rest of the family is all in the same leaky craft. Carruthers put Sallie's in himself, but I invested the mites belonging to the others. Of course, as far as the old folks are concerned, I can more than take care of them, and if anything happens there's enough life insurance and to spare for them. I don't feel exactly responsible for Sallie's situation, but I do feel the responsibility of their helplessness. Sallie is not fitted to cope with the world and she ought to be well provided for. I feel that more and more every day. Her helplessness is very beautiful and tender, but in a way tragic, don't you think?"

I wish I had dared tell him for the second time that day what I did think on the subject but I denied myself such frankness.

Anyway, men are just stupid, faithful children - some of them faithful, I mean.

I felt that if I stood there talking with the Crag any longer, I might grow pedagogical and teach him a few things so I sent him home across the road. I knew all six women would stay awake until they heard him lock them in, come down to the lodge and lock his own door.

It is very unworthy of me to enjoy his playing a watch-dog of tradition across the road to an emancipated woman like myself. The situation both keeps me awake and puts me to sleep - and it is sweet, though I don't know why.

God never made anything more wonderful than a good
man, - even a stupid one. Lights out!

Maria Thompson Daviess

CHAPTER VI

MAX AND THE ASAFETIDA SPOON

I do wish the great man who is discovering how to put people into some sort of metaphysical pickle that will suspend their animations until he gets ready to wake them up, would hurry up with his investigations, so he can catch Sallie before she begins to fade or wilt. Sallie, just as she is, brought to life about five generations from now, would cause a sensation.

Some women are so feminine that they are sticky, unless well spiced with deviltry. Sallie's loveliness hasn't much seasoning. Still, I do love her dearly, and I am just as much her slave as are any of the others. I can't get out of it.

"Do you suppose we will ever get all of the clothes done for the twins?" Nell sighed gently as we sat on my porch whipping yards of lace upon white ruffles and whipping up our own spirits at the same time. Everybody in Glendale sews for Sallie's children and it takes her all her time to think up the clothes.

"Never," I answered.

"She's coming, and I do believe she has got more of this ruffling. I see it floating down her skirt," Nell fairly groaned.

Nell ought to like to sew. She isn't emancipated enough to hate a needle as I do. But the leaven is working and she's rising slowly. It might be well for some man to work the dough down a little before she runs over the pan. That's a primitively feminine wish and not at all in accordance with my own advanced ideas.

I was becoming slightly snarled with my thread, and I was glad when Sallie and her sweetness seated itself in the best rocker in the softest breeze, which Nell had vacated for her.

"Children are the greatest happiness in life and also the greatest responsibility, girls," she said, in her lovely rich voice that always melts me to a solution of sympathy whenever she uses it pensively on me. "Of course, I should be desolate without mine, but what could I do with them, if I didn't have all of you dear people to help me with them?"

Her wistful dependence had charm.

I looked at the twin with the yellow fuzz on the top of its head that has hall-marked it as the Kitten in my mind, seated on Sallie's lap with her head on Sallie's shoulder looking like a baby bud folded against the full rose, and I couldn't help laughing. Kit had been undressed three times after her bath this morning while Cousin Martha, Cousin Jasmine and Mrs. Hargrove argued with each other whether she should or shouldn't have a scrap of flannel put on over her fat little stomach. Henrietta finally decided the matter by being impudent and sensible to them all about the temperature.

"Don't you all 'spose God made the sun some to heat up Kit's stomach?" she demanded scornfully, as she grabbed the little roly-poly bone of contention and marched off with her to finish dressing her on the front porch in the direct rays of her instituted heater.

The household at large at Widegables can never agree on the clothing of the twins and Henrietta often has to finish their toilets thus, by force. Aunt Dilsie being reduced by her phthisic to a position that is almost entirely orna-mental, Henrietta's strength of character is the only thing that has made the existence of the twins bearable to themselves or other people.

As I have said before, I do wish that some day in the future you will come under the direct rays of Henrietta's influence, Jane, dear!

"Yes, Sallie, I should call them a responsibility," I answered her with a laugh, as I reached up my arms for the Kitten. Then, as the little yellow head snuggled in the hollow that was instituted in the beginning between a woman's breast and arm for the purpose of just such nestlings, I whispered as I laid my lips against her little ear, "and a happiness, too, darling."

And as Sallie rocked and recuperated her breath Nell eyed the ruffle apprehensively.

"Are you going to let us make another dress for the kiddies, Sallie, dear?" she finally was forced by her uneasiness to ask, though with the deepest sweetness and consideration in her voice.

If I am ever a widow with young children I hope they will burn us all up with the deceased rather than keep me wrapped in a cotton-wool of sympathy, as all of us do Sallie.

"It's lovely of you, Nell, to want to do more for the babies after all the beautiful things you and Evelina have made them, and I may be able to get another white dress apiece for them after I give Cousin James the bills, that are awful already, but this is some ruffling that I just forced Mamie Hall to let me bring up to you girls to do for her baby. The poor little dear is two months old and Mamie is just beginning on his little dress for him. He has been wearing the plainest little slips. Mamie says Ned remarked on the fact that the baby was hardly presentable when you girls stopped in with him to see it the other day, Nell. I urged her to get right to work fixing him up. It is wrong for children not to be kept as daintily as their father likes to see them."

How any woman that is as spiritually-minded as I am, and who has so much love for the whole world in her heart, and such a deep purpose always to offer it to her fellowmen according to their need of it, can have the vile temper I possess I cannot see.

"And the sight that would please me better than anything else I have even thought up to want to see," I found myself saying when I became conscious - I hope I didn't use any of the oaths of my forefathers which must have been tempting my refined foremothers for generations and which I secretly admire Henrietta for indulging in on occasions of impatience with Sallie - "would be Ned Hall left entirely alone with that squirming baby, that looks exactly like him, when it is having a terrible spell of colic and Ned is in the midst of a sick headache, with all the other children cold, hungry, and cross, the cook gone to a funeral, and the nurse in a grouch because she couldn't go and - and he knowing that Mamie was attired in a lovely, cool muslin dress, sitting up here on the porch with us sipping a mint julep and smoking a ten-cent cigar, resting and getting up an appetite for supper. I want him to have about five years of such days and then he would deserve the joys of parenthood that he now does not appreciate."

"Oh, Mamie wouldn't smoke a cigar!" was the exclamation that showed how much Sallie got of the motif of my eruption.

"Glorious!" exclaimed Nell, with shining eyes.

I must be careful about Nell, she is going this new gait too fast for one so young. Women must learn to fletcherize freedom if it is not to give them indigestion of purpose.

"Still Ned provides everything in the world he can think of to help Mamie," said Caroline, who had come up the walk just in time to fan the flame in me by her sweet wistfulness, with a soft judiciousness in her voice and eyes. "And Mamie adores the children and him."

If one man is unattainable to a woman all the other creatures take on the hue of being valuable from the reflection. Caroline is pathetic!

"It would be robbing a woman of a privilege not to let her trot the colic out of her own baby," Sallie got near enough in sight of the discussion to shout softly from the rear.

I have often seen Cousin Martha on one side of the fire trotting the Pup, and Cousin Jasmine on the other ministrating likewise to the Kit. so Sallie could take a good nap, which she didn't at all need, on the long sofa in the living-room at Widegables.

"Ned is a delightful man and, of course, Mamie adores him." Nell agreed with an attitude of mind like to the attitude of a body sustained on the top rail of a shaky fence.

"He doubtless would be just as delightful to Mamie standing by dropping asafetida into a spoon to administer to the baby, as he is dancing with you at the Assembly, Nell," I said, still frothy around the temper.

"He'll never do it again," was the prompt result I got from my shot.

"The trouble with you, Evelina," said Sallie, with ruminative reflectiveness in her eyes, "is that you have never been married and do not understand how noble a man can be under - "

"Yes, I should say that you had hit Evelina's trouble exactly on the head, Sallie," came in Polk's drawl as he came over the rose hedge from the side street and seated himself beside Caroline on the steps.

"Well, if I ever have a husband he'll prove his nobility by being competent to make the correct connection between the asafetida spoon and his own baby," was the answer that came with so much force that I couldn't stop it after I fully realized Folk's presence and sex.

"Help!" exclaimed Polk, weakly, while Nell blushed into the fold of her ruffle, Caroline looked slightly shocked and Sallie wholly scandalized at my lack of delicacy.

I felt that the place had been reached, the audience provided, and the time ripe for the first gun in my general revolution planned for Glendale. I spoke calmly in a perfect panic of fear.

"I am glad Polk is here to speak for the masculine side of the question," I said, looking all the three astonished women straight in the face. "Polk, do you or do you not think that a man with a wife and seven children ought to assume at least some of the domestic strain resulting therefrom, like dropping the asafetida in the spoon for her while she is wrestling with the youngest-born's colic?"

"Do I have to answer?" pleaded Polk, with desperation.

"Yes!"

"Then, under the circumstances I think the man ought to say: 'To hell with the spoon,' grab a gun, go out and shoot up a bear and a couple of wild turkeys for breakfast, throttle some coin out of some nearby business corporation, send two to five trained nurses back to the wigwam, stay down town to lunch and then go home with a tender little kiss for the madame who meets him fluffy and smiling at the door. That's my idea of true connubial bliss. Applications considered in the order of their reception. Nell, you are sweet enough to eat in that blue muslin. I'm glad I asked you to get one just that shade!"

And the inane chorus of pleased laughs that followed Polk Hayes's brainless disposal of the important question in hand made me ashamed of being a woman - though it was funny. Still I bided my time and Polk saw the biding, I could tell by the expression in the corners of his eyes that he kept turned away from me.

And in less than a half-hour he was left to my mercies, anything but tender. Sallie took Nell and Caroline over home to help her decide how wide a band of white it would be decorous for her to sew in the neck of her new black meteor crepe. I see it coming that we will all have to unite in getting Sallie out of mourning and into the trappings of frivolity soon and I dread it. It takes so many opinions on any given subject to satisfy Sallie that she ought to keep a tabulated advice-book.

"Evelina," said Polk, experimentally, after he had seen them safely across the street, and he moved along the steps until he sat against my skirts, "are your family subject to colic?"

"No, they have strong brains instead," I answered icily.

"Said brains subject to colic, though," he mused in an impudent undertone.

I laughed: I couldn't help it. One of the dangerous things about Polk is that he gets you comfortable and warm of heart whenever he gets near you. It wouldn't matter at all to him if you should freeze later for lack of his warmth, just so he doesn't know about it.

"Polk," I began to say in a lovely serious tone of voice, looking him square in the eyes and determined that as we were now on the subject of basic things, like infantile colic, I would have it out with him along all lines, "there is an awful shock coming to you when you realize that - "

"That in the heat of this erudite and revolutionary discussion, which an evil fate led me to drop in on, I have forgotten to give you this telegram that came for you while I was down at the station shipping some lumber. Be as easy as you can with me, Evelina, and remember that I am your childhood's companion when you decide between us." With which he handed me a blue telegram.

I opened it hastily and found that it was from Richard:

> Am coming down to Bolivar with C. & G. Commission. Be deciding about what I wrote you. Must.
>
> RICHARD.

I sat perfectly still for several seconds because I felt that a good strong hand had reached out of the distance and gently grabbed me. Dickie had bossed me strenuously through two years of the time before I had awakened to the fact that, for his good, I must take the direction of the affairs of him and his kind on my and my kind's shoulders.

I suppose a great many years of emancipation will have to pass over the heads of women before they lose the gourd kind of feeling at the sight of a particularly broad, strong pair of shoulders. My heart sparkled at the idea of seeing Dickie again and being browbeaten in a good old, methodical, tender way. I suppose the sparkle in my heart showed in my eyes, for Polk sat up quickly and took notice of it very decidedly.

"Wire especially impassioned?" he asked, with a smolder in his eyes.

"Not especially." I answered serenely, "One of my friend's father is a director in the C. & G. and he is coming down with him for the conference over at Bolivar between the two roads next week."

"Good," answered Polk, heartily, as the flare died out of his eyes.

I was glad he didn't have to see the wire for I wanted to use Polk's brain a while if I could get his emotions to sleep in my presence. It is very exasperating for a woman to be offered flirtation when she is in need of common sense from a man. There are so many times she needs the one rather than the other, but the dear creatures refuse to realize it, if she's under forty.

"Polk, do you see any logical, honest or dishonest way to

get that Road to take the Glendale bluff line?" I asked, with trepidation, for that was the first time I had ever even begun to discuss anything intelligently with Polk.

"None in the world, Evelina," he answered with a nice, straight, intellectuality showing over his whole face and even his lazy, posing figure. "I remonstrated with James and Henry Carruthers both when they used their influence to have the bonds voted and I told James it was madness to invest in all that field and swamp property with just a chance of the shops. The trouble was that James had always left all his business to Henry, along with the firm's business, for a man can't be the kind of lawyer James is, and carry the details of the handling of filthy lucre in the same mind that can make a speech like the one he made down in Nashville last April, on the exchange of the Judiciary. James can be the Governor of this good State any time he wants to, or could, if Henry hadn't turned toes and left him such a bag to hold - no reference to Sallie's figure intended, which is all to the good if you like that kind of curves!"

I took a moment to choose my words.

"The C. & G. is going to take that bluff route," I answered calmly from somewhere inside me that I had never used to speak from before.

"Do you know anything of the character of Mrs. Joshua?" asked Polk, admiringly, but slipping down from his intellectual attitude of mind and body and edging an inch nearer. "Bet she had a strong mind or Joshua never could have pulled off that sun and moon stunt."

"Do you know, Polk, there is one woman in the world who could - could handle you?" I said, as a sudden vision of what Jane would do, if Polk sat on her skirts as he did on mine, flashed across my troubled brain.

"I'd be mighty particular as to who handles me," he answered impudently, "Want to try?" And with the greatest audacity he laid his head gently against my knee. I let it rest there a second and then tipped it back against the arm of the rocker.

"It does hurt me to see a man like Cousin James fairly throttled by women as he is being," I said as I looked across the street and noted that the porch of Widegables was full to overflowing with the household of women.

"Evelina," said Polk, as he stood up suddenly in front of me, "that old Mossback is the finest man in this commonwealth, but from his situation nobody can extract him, unless it is a woman with the wiliness of the devil himself. Poison the whole bunch and I'll back you. But we'll have to plot it later on. I see his reverence coming tripping along with a tract in his hand for you and I'll be considerate enough to sneak through the kitchen, get a hot muffin-cake that has been tantalizing my nose all this time you have been sentimentalizing over me, and return anon when I can have you all to myself in the melting moonlight in the small hours after all religious folk are in bed. Until then!" And as he went back through the front hall Mr. Haley came down the front walk.

"My dear Miss Shelby, how fortunate I am to find you alone," he exclaimed with such genuine delight beaming from his nice, good, friendly, gray eyes that I beamed up myself a bit out of pure responsiveness.

"I am so glad to see you, Mr. Haley. Hasn't it been a lovely day?" I answered, as I offered him the large rocker Sallie had vacated.

"It has, indeed, and I don't know when I have been as deeply happy. This hour with you will be the very climax of the day's perfections, I feel sure."

I smiled.

To follow you, Jane, I "let a man look freely into my heart and thus encouraged he opened his to mine" and behold, I found Sallie and the twins and Henrietta all squatting in the Dominie's cardiac regions, just as comfortably as they do it at Widegables.

"My sympathies have become so enlisted in the struggle which Mrs. Carruthers is having to curb the eccentricities of her oldest daughter that I feel I must lay definite plans to help her. It is very difficult for a young and naturally yielding woman like Mrs. Carruthers to discipline alone even so young a child as Henrietta. I know you will help me all you can to help her. Believe me, my dear friend, even in the short time you have been in Glendale you have become a tower of strength to me. I feel that I can take my most difficult and sacred perplexities to you."

Now, what do you think of that, Jane? Be sure and rub this situation in on all the waiting Five disciples. I defy any of them to do so well in less than three months. This getting on a plane of common citizenship with a fellow-man is easy. That is, with some men.

Still while you are getting on the plane somebody else gets the man. What about that? I didn't want Mr. Haley, but what if I had?

"Yes, Henrietta is a handful, Mr. Haley," I answered with enthusiasm, for even the mention of Henrietta enlivens me and somehow Mr. Haley's getting in the game of "curbing" her stirred up my risibles. "But - but Sallie already has a good many people to help her with the children. I have been trying to - to influence Henrietta - and she does not swear except on the most exasperating occasions now."

"The dear little child created a slight consternation in her Sunday School class last week when they were being taught the great dramatic story of Jonah's three days' incarceration in the whale. To quote her exactly, so that you may see how it must have affected the other children, she said: 'I swallowed a live fly onct myself and I'm not damn fool enough to believe that whale kept Jonah down three days, alive and kicking, no matter who says so.'

"She then marched out of the class and has not returned these two succeeding Sabbaths. It was to talk over the matter I called on Mrs. Carruthers this afternoon, and I have never had my sympathies so stirred. We must help her, my dear friend!"

I never enjoyed anything more in my life than the hour I spent helping that dear, good, funny man plan first aids to the rearing of Sallie's children. Besides my cooeeration he has planned to enlist that of Aunt Augusta, and I was wicked enough to let him do it. In a small village where the inhabitants have no chance at diversions like Wagnerian operas and collapsing skyscrapers I felt that I had no right to avert the spectacle of Aunt Augusta's disciplining Henrietta.

I'll write you all about it, Jane, in a special delivery letter.

Jasper whipped Petunia with great apparent severity day before yesterday, and we have been having the most heavenly waffles and broiled chicken ever since. I dismissed Jasper for doing it, but Petunia came into my room and cried about it a half-hour, so I had to go out where he was rubbing the silver and forgive him and hire him over.

"When a woman gits her mouth stuck out at a man and the world in general three days hand running they ain't nothing to cure it but a stick," he answered with lofty scorn.

"Yes'm, dat's so," answered Petunia. "I never come outen a spell so easy before." And her yellow face had a pink glow of happiness all over it as she smiled lovably on the black brute.

I went off into a corner and sat down for a quiet hour to think. Nobody in the world knows everything.

"Supper's on the table," Jasper announced, after having seen Mr. Haley go down the front walk to-night. Jasper has such great respect for the cloth that never in the world would he have asked Mr. Haley in to supper without having at least a day to prepare for him. Any of my other friends he would have asked, regardless of whether or not I wanted them.

I somehow didn't feel that I could eat alone to-night, but it was too late to go for Sallie or Cousin Jasmine, and besides it is weak-minded to feel that way. Why shouldn't I want to eat by myself?

This is a great big house for just one woman, and I don't see why I have to be that one! I never was intended to be single. I seem to even think double. Way down in me there is a place that all my life I have been laying things aside in to tell some day to somebody that will understand. I don't remember a single one of them now, but when the time comes somebody is going to ask me a question very softly and it is going to be the key that will unlock the treasures of all my life, and he will take them out one by one, and look at them and love them and smile over them and scold over them and be frightened even to swearing over them, perhaps weep over them, and then - while I'm very close - pray over them. I could feel the tears getting tangled in my lashes, but I forced them back.

Now, I don't see why I should have been sentimentalizing over myself like that. Just such a longing, miserable, wait-until-he-comes - and why-doesn't-he-hurry-or-I'll-take-the-wrong-man attitude of mind and sentiment in women in general is what I have taken a vow on my soul, and made a great big important wager to do away with. There are millions of lovely men in the world and all I have to do is to go out and find the right one, be gentle with him until he understands my mode of attack to be a bit different from the usual crawfish one employed by women from prehistoric times until now, but not later: and then domesticate him in any way that suits me.

Here I've been in Glendale almost three months and have let my time be occupied keeping house for nobody but myself and to entertain my friends, planting a flower garden that can't be used at all for nourishment, and sewing on another woman's baby clothes.

I've written millions of words in this book and there is as yet not one word that will help the Five in the serious and important task of proving that they have a right to choose their own mates, and certainly nothing to help them perform the ceremonial.

If I don't do better than this Jane will withdraw her offer and there is no telling how many years the human race will be retarded by my lack of strength of character.

What do men do when they begin to see the gray hairs on

their temples and when they have been best-man at twenty-three weddings, and are tired of being at christenings and buying rattles, and things at the club all taste exactly alike, and they have purchased ten different kinds of hair-tonic that it bores them to death to rub on the tops of their own heads?

I don't want any man I know! I might want Polk, if I let him have half a chance to make me, but that would be dishonorable.

I've got up so much nice warm sisterly love for Dickie and Mr. Haley that I couldn't begin to love them in the right way now, I am afraid. Still, I haven't seen Dickie for three months and maybe my desperation will have the effect of enhancing his attractions. I hope so.

Still I am disgusted deeply with myself. I believe if I could experiment with mankind I could make some kind of creature that would be a lot better than a woman for all purposes, and I would -

"Supper's ready and company come," Jasper came to the front door to announce for the third time, but this time with the unctuous voice of delight that a guest always inspires in him. I promptly went in to welcome my materialized desire whoever it happened to be.

The Crag was standing by the window in the half light that came, partly from the candles in their tall old silver candlesticks that were Grandmother Shelby's, and partly from the last glow of the sun down over the ridge. That was what I needed!

"I was coming in from the fields across your back yard and I saw the table lighted and you on the front porch, star-gazing, and - and I got Jasper to invite me." he said as he came over and drew out my chair on one side of that wide square table, while Jasper stood waiting to seat him at the other, about a mile away.

"I wanted you," I answered him stupidly, as I sank into my place and leaned my elbows on the table so I could drop my warm cheeks into my hands comfortably. I didn't see why I should be blushing.

"That's the reason I came then," he answered, as he looked at me across the bowl of musk roses that were sending out waves of sweetness to meet those that were coming in from the honeysuckle climbing over the window. "If you were ever lonely and needed me, Evelina, you would tell me, wouldn't you?" he asked, as he leaned towards me and regarded me still more closely.

And again those two treacherous tears rose and tangled themselves in my lashes, though I did shake them away quickly as a smile quivered its way to command of my mouth. But I was not quick enough and he saw them.

And what he did was just what I wanted him to do! He rose, picked up his chair and came around that huge old table and sat down at the corner just as near to my elbow as the steaming coffee pot would let him.

"If you wanted me any time, would you tell me, Evelina?" he insisted from this closer range.

"No, I wouldn't," I answered with a laugh. "I would expect you to know it, and come just like you did to-night."

"But - but it was I that wanted you badly in this case," he answered with an echo of the laugh.

But even under the laugh I saw signs of excitement in his deep eyes and his long, lean hands shook as they handed me his cup to pour the coffee. Jasper had laid his silver and napkin in front of him and retired to admonish Petunia as to the exact crispness of her first waffle.

"What is it?" I asked breathlessly, as I moved the coffee pot from between us to the other side.

"Just a letter that came to me from the Democratic Headquarters in the City, that shook me up a bit and made me want to - to tell *you* about it. Nobody else can know - I have been out on Old Harpeth all afternoon fighting that out, and telling you is the only thing I have allowed myself."

"They want you to be the next Governor," I said quickly. "And you will be, too," I added, again using that queer place in my brain that seems to know perfectly unknowable things and that only works in matters that concern him.

"No!"

"Yes, Your Excellency," I hurled at him defiantly.

"You witch, you," he answered me with a pleased, teasing whimsicality coming into his eyes. "Of course, you guessed the letter and it was dear to have you do it, but we both know it is impossible. Nobody must hear of it, and the telling you has been the best I could get out of it anyway. Jasper, take my compliments to Petunia, this chicken is perfection!"

That eighth wonder of the world which got lost was something even more mysterious than the Sphinx. It was a marvel that could have been used for women to compare men to. That man sat right there at my side and ate four waffles, two large pieces of chicken and a liver-wing, drank two cups of coffee, and then devoured a huge bowl of peaches and cream, with three muffin-cakes, while enduring the tragedy of the realization of having to decline the Governorship of his State.

I watched him do it, first in awe and then with a dim understanding of something, I wasn't sure what. Most women, under the circumstances, would have gone to bed and cried it out or at least have refused food for hours. We've got to get over those habits before we get to the point of having to refuse to be Governors of the States and railroad presidents and things like that.

And while he ate, there I sat not able to more than nibble because I was making up my mind to do something that scared me to death to think about. That gaunt, craggy man in a shabby gray coat, cut ante-bellum wise, with a cravat that wound itself around his collar, snowy and dainty, but on the same lines as the coat and evidently of rural manufacture in the style favored by the flower and chivalry of the day of Henry Clay, had progressive me as completely overawed for several minutes as any painted redskin ever dominated a squaw - or as Jasper did Petunia in my own kitchen.

But after we were left alone with the roses and the candles and his cigar, with only Jasper's gratified voice mumbling over compliments to Petunia in the distance, I took my courage in my hands and plunged.

This can he used as data for the Five.

"James." I said, with such cool determination in my voice that it almost froze my own tongue, "I meant to tell you about it several weeks ago, I have decided to adopt Sallie and all the children. I intend to legally adopt the children and just nominally adopt Sallie, but it will amount to the same thing. I don't have to have your consent but I think it is courteous to ask for it."

"What!" he exclaimed, as he sat up and looked at me with the expression an alienist might use in an important examination.

"Yes," I answered, gaining courage with time. "You see, I was crying out here on the porch with loneliness when you found me. I can't stand this any longer. I must have a family right away and Sallie's just suits me. I have to take a great deal of interest in them anyway and it would be easier if I had complete control of them. It will leave you with enough family to keep you from being lonely and then we can all be happy together down into old age."

"Have you said anything about this to Sallie?" he asked weakly as he dipped the end of his cigar into his glass of water and watched the sputter with the greatest interest.

"Not yet, but don't you feel sure that she will consent?" I asked, with confidence in my plan at fever heat. "Sallie is so generous and she can't want to see me live lonely always, without any family at all. Now, will she?"

"She would consent!" he answered slowly, and then he laid his head down on the table right against my arm and shook so that the candlesticks rattled against the candles. "But I don't," he gasped, and for the life of me I couldn't tell whether he was crying or laughing, until he sat up again.

"Eve," he said, with his eyes fairly dancing into mine, "if women in general mean to walk over political difficulties as you are planning to walk away with this one of mine,

I'm for feminine rule. Don't you dare say one word about such a thing to Sallie. Of course, it is impossible as it is funny."

It was a tragedy to have such a lovely scheme as I had thought up on the spur of the moment, knocked down suddenly by a half dozen positive words from a mere man, and for a moment my eyes fought with his in open rebellion. Then I rose haughtily and walked out on the front porch.

"Dear," he said, as he followed me and took my hand in his and drew me near him, "don't you know that your wanting to put your shoulder under any burden I may be bearing lifts it completely? There are things in this situation that you can't understand. If I seem to make sacrifices, they come from the depths of my heart and are not sacrifices. Will you believe me?"

How can he help loving Sallie with her so emphatically there?

I answered him I suppose to his liking and he went on across the road to Widegables and left me alone in the cruel darkness.

Please, God, when things seem to be drowning me like this make me swim with head up. Amen!

CHAPTER VII

SOME SMOLDERINGS

I'm a failure! Yes, Jane, I am!

Polk Hayes is an up-to-date, bright man of the world, with lots of brains and I should say about the average masculine nature, and a great deal more than the average amount of human charm. However, he has got no more brains than I have, has had really fewer advantages, and it ought to be easy for me to hold my own against him. But I am about to fail on him.

For the last two weeks he has been constantly with Nell and has got her in a dreamy state that shows in her face and every movement of her slim body. And yet I know without the shadow of a doubt that he is just biding his time to try me out and get me on his own terms. My heart aches for Nell, and I just couldn't see him murder her girlhood, and it will amount to that if he involves her heart any more than it is. I made up my mind to have it out with him and accordingly let him come and sit on my side steps with me late yesterday afternoon, when I have avoided being alone with him for a month.

"Polk," I asked him suddenly without giving him time to get the situation into his own hands, skilled in their woman-handling, "do you intend to marry Nell or just plain break her heart for the fun you get out of it?"

His dangerous eyes smoldered back at me for a long minute before he answered me:

"Men don't break women's hearts, Evelina."

"I think you are right," I answered slowly, "they do just wring and distort them and deform them for life. But I intend to see that Nell's has no such torturous operation performed on it if I can appeal to you or convince her."

"When you argue with Nell be sure and don't tell her just exactly the things *you* have done to *me* all this summer through, Evelina." He answered coolly.

"What do you mean?" I demanded, positively cold with a kind of astonished fear.

"I mean that I have never offered Nell one half of the torture you have offered me, every day since you came home, with your damned affectionate friendliness. When I laugh, you answer it before it gets articulate, and when I gloom, you are as sympathetic as sympathy itself. I have held your hand and kissed it, instituting and not quenching a raging thirst thereby, as you are experienced enough to know. You have made yourself everything for me that is responsive and desirable and beautiful and worthy and have put me back every time I have reached out to grasp you. You don't want me, you don't want to marry me at all, you just want - excitement. You are as cold as ice that grinds and generates fire. Very well, you don't have to take me - and I'll get what I can from Nell - and others."

"Oh, Polk, how could you have misunderstood me like this?" I moaned from the depths of an almost broken heart. But as I moaned I understood - I understood!

I'm doing it all wrong! I had the most beautiful human love for him in my heart and he thought it was all dastardly, cold coquetting. An awful spark has been struck out of the flint. I'm not worthy to experiment with this dreadful man-and-woman question. I just laid my head down on my arms, resting on my knees and cowered at Polk's feet.

"Don't - Evelina, I didn't mean it." he said quickly in a shaken voice. But he did!

I couldn't answer him and as I sat still and prayed in my heart for some words to come that would do away with the horror I heard Sallie's voice from my front walk, and she and Mr. Haley, each carrying a sleeping twin, came around the corner of the porch.

That interruption was a direct answer to prayer, for God knew that I just must have time to think before having this out with Polk. I sometimes feel ashamed of the catastrophes I have to pray quick about, but what would I do if I couldn't?

I don't know how I got through the rest of this evening, but I did - I pray for sleep. Amen!

Watching the seasons follow each other in the Harpeth Valley gives me the agony of a dumb poet, who can feel though not sing.

It was spring when I came down here four months ago, a young, tender, mist-veiled, lilac-scented spring that nestled firmly in your heart and made it ache with sweetness that you hardly understood yourself.

But before I knew it the young darling, with her curls and buds and apple-blooms had gone and summer was rioting over the gardens and fields and hills, rich, lush colored, radiant, redolent, gorgeous, rose-scented and pulsing with a life that made me breathless. Even the roads along the valley were bordered with flowers that the sun had wooed to the swooning point.

But this week, early as it is, there has been a hint of autumn in the air, and a haze is beginning to creep over the whole world, especially in the early mornings, which are so dew-gemmed that they seem to be hinting a warning of the near coming of frost and snow.

My garden has grown into a perfect riot of blooms, but for the last two weeks queer slugs have begun to eat the tender buds that are forming for October blooming, and I have been mourning over it by day and by night and to everybody who will listen.

Aunt Augusta insists that the only thing to do is to get up with the first crack of dawn and carefully search out each slug, remove it and destroy it. She says if this is done for a week they will be exterminated.

I carefully explained it all to Jasper and when I came down to breakfast he was coming in with three queer green things, also with an injured air of having been kept up all night. I didn't feel equal to making him go on with the combat and ignored the question for two days until I saw all the buds on my largest Neron done for in one night.

I have always been able to get up at the break of day to go sketching - it was at daybreak that I made my sketch in the Defleury gardens that captured the French art eye enough to get me my Salon mention. If I could get up to splash water-colors at that hour, I surely could rush to the protection of my own roses, so I went to bed with gray dawn on my mind and the shutters wide open so the first light would get full in my eyes.

I am glad that it was a good bright ray that woke me and partly dazzled me, for the sight I had, after I had been kneeling down in the rose bed for fifteen minutes, was something of a shock to me, though no reason in the world why it should have been. I can't remember that I ever speculated as to whether the Crag wore pajamas or not, and I don't see that I should have been surprised that he did instead of the night shirt of our common ancestry.

He came around the side of the house out of the sun-shot mist and was half way down the garden path before I saw him or he saw me, and I must say that his unconcern under the circumstances was rather remarkable.

He was attired in a light blue silk pajama jacket that was open at the throat and half way down his broad breast. He had on his usual gray trousers, but tag's of blue trailed out and ruffled around his bare ankles, and across his bare heels that protruded from his slippers. His hair was in heavy tousled black curls all over his head and his gray eyes were positively mysterious with interrupted dreams. In one hand he carried a tin can and in the other a small pointed stick, which looked murderously fitted for the extermination of the marauders.

I was positively nervous over the prospect of his embarrassment when he should catch sight of me, but there was none.

"Eve!" he exclaimed, with surprise, and a ray of pure delight drove away the dreams in his eyes. Nobody in the wide world calls me Eve but just the Crag, and he does it in a queer, still way when he is surprised to see me, or glad, or sorry, or moved with any kind of sudden emotion.

And queer as it is I have to positively control the desire to answer him with the correlated title - Adam!

"I forgot to tell you yesterday that I was coming over to get the slugs for you, dear," he said as he came down the row of roses next to mine, squatted opposite to where I was kneeling by the bushy, suffering Neron and began to examine the under side of each leaf carefully. He was the most beautiful thing I have ever seen in the early light with his great chest bare and the blue of the pajamas melting into the bronze of his throat and calling out the gray in his eyes. I had to force myself into being gardener rather than artist, as we laughed together over the glass bowl and silver spoon I had brought out for the undoing of the slugs. Some day I'm going to paint him like that!

I found out about the pajamas from questioning Aunt Martha discreetly. They seemed so incongruous in relation to the usual old Henry Clay coat and stock collar, that I had to know the reason why. Mrs. Hargrove's son was a very worldly man, she says, and wore them. It comforts her to make them for the Crag to wear in memoriam. He wears the collars Cousin Martha makes him with her own fingers after the pattern she made his father's by, for the same reason, and lets Cousin Jasmine cut his hair because she always cut her father's, Colonel Horton's, until his death. That accounts for the ante-bellum curls and the irregular tags in the back. I almost laughed when Cousin Martha was telling me, but I remembered how a glow rose in my heart when I saw that he still had Father's little old Confederate comrade tailor cut his coats on the same pattern on which he had cut Father's, since the days of reconstruction. Sometimes it startles me to find that with all my emancipation I am very like other women.

But I wonder what I would do if Sallie attired him in any

of the late Henry's wearing apparel?

"What do you suppose is the why of such useless things as slugs?" I speculated to stop that thought off sharp as we crawled down the row together, he searching one side of each bush and I the other.

"Well, they brought on this nice companionable hunt for them, didn't they?" he asked, looking over into my eyes with a laugh.

"I wanted to see you early this morning anyway," he hastily resumed. "Sallie and the Dominie sat talking to you so late last night that I didn't feel it was fair to come across after they left. But I wanted you so I could hardly get to sleep, and I was just half awake from a dream of you, when I came into the garden."

"My evenings don't belong to anybody, if you need them, Jamie, and you don't have to be told that," I answered crossly when I thought what a grand time I might have been having talking about real things with the Crag, instead of wrestling with Polk's romantics or Sallie's and Mr. Haley's gush.

"Go on and tell me all about it, while I crawl after you like a worm myself," I snapped still further.

"Well, here goes! In the City Council meeting last night your Uncle Peter told us about the plans that they have made up at Bolivar for entertaining the C. & G. Commission, and the gloom of Polk and Lee, Ned and the rest of them could have easily been cut in blocks and used for cold storage purposes. They are just all down and out about it and no fight left. Of course, they all lose by the bond issue, but I can't see that it is bad enough to knock them all out like this. I got up in mighty wrath and - and I have got myself into one job. My eloquence landed me right into one large hole, and I am reaching out for a hand from you."

"Here it is," and I reached over and left a smear of loam across the back of his hand, while I brought away a brown circle around my wrist that the responsive grasp of his fingers left. "Do you want me single-handed to get the bluff line chosen?"

"Not quite, but almost," he answered with another laugh. "You would if you tried. I haven't a doubt. Do you remember the talk we had the other night about its seeming inhospitable of you not to invite the other gentlemen in the Commission over to see you when you invite Hall and his father? And you know you had partly planned some sort of entertainment for the whole bunch. You had the right idea at the right place, as you always do. As you said, we don't want Bolivar to see us with what looks like a grouch on us at their good fortune, and I think that as the Commission are all to be here as the guests of a private citizen, Glendale ought to entertain them publicly. There is no hope to get the line for us, but I would like those men at least to see what the beauty of that bluff road would be. The line across the river runs through the only ugly part of the valley, and while I know in the balance between dollars and scenery, scenery will go down and out, still it would be good for them to see it and at least get a vision of what might have been, to haunt them when they take their first trip through the swamps across the country there. Now, as you are to have them anyway, I want to have the whole town entertain the whole Commission and Bolivar with what is classically called among us a barbecue-rally, the countryside to be invited. Bolivar is going to give them a banquet, to be as near like what the Bolivarians imagine they have in New York as possible, and Mrs. Doctor Henderson is to give them a pink tea reception to which carefully chosen presentables, like you and me, are to be invited. You remember that circus day in July? - a rally will be like that or more so. What do you think?"

"Oh, I think you are a genius to think about it," I gasped, as I sat down on a very cruet Killarney branch and just as quickly sat up again, receiving comforting expressions of sympathy from across the bush, to which I paid no heed. "Those blase city men will go crazy about it. We can have the barbecue up on the bluff, where we have always had it for the political rallies, and a fish-fry and the country people in their wagons with children tumbling all over everything and - and you will make a great speech with all of us looking on and being proud of you, because nobody in New York or beyond can do as well. We can invite a lot of people up from the City and over from Bolivar and Hillsboro and Providence to hear you tell them all about Tennessee while things are cooking and - "

"This rally is to show off Glendale not - the Crag," he interrupted me with a quizzical laugh.

Now, how did he know I called him the Crag in my heart? I suppose I did it to his face and never knew. I seem to think right out loud when I am with him and feel out loud, too. I ignored his levity, that was out of place when he saw how my brain was beginning to work well and rapidly.

"You mean, don't you, Jamie, that you want to get Glendale past this place that is - humiliating - swimming with her head up?" I asked softly past a rose that drooped against my cheek.

Perfectly justifiable tears came to my lashes as I thought what a humiliation it all was to him and the rest of them, to be passed by an opportunity like that and left to die in their gray moldiness off the main line of life - shelved.

"That is one of my prayers, to get past humiliations, swimming with my head up," I added softly, though I blushed from my toes to my top curl at the necessity that had called out the prayer the last time. It's awful on a woman to feel herself growing up stiff and sturdy by a man's side and then to get sight of a gourd-vine tangling itself up between them. I'm the dryad out of one of my own twin oaks down by the gate, and I want the other twin to be -

I wonder if his eyes really look to other women like deep gray pools that you can look deeper and deeper into and never seem to get to the bottom, no matter if the look does seem to last forever and you feel yourself blushing and wanting to take your eyes away, or if it is just I that get so drowned in them!

"You've a gallant stroke, Evelina," he said softly, as I at last gained possession of my own sight. "And here I am with a hand out to you for assistance in carrying out your own plan that seems to be just the thing to - "

"Say, Cousin James. Aunt Marfy says for you to come home to breakfast right away. Mis' Hargrove won't let nobody begin until you says the blessing, and Cousin Jasmine have got the headache from waiting for her coffee. What do you want to fool with Evelina this time of day for anyway?" And with the delivery of which message and reproof Henrietta stood on the edge of the path looking down upon us with great and scornful interest.

"You've got on your night shirt and haven't combed your hair or washed your face," she continued sternly. "There'll be hell to pay with all the breakfast getting cold, and I'm empty down to my feet. Come on, quick!"

"Henrietta," I said, sternly, as I rose to my feet, "I've asked you once not to say ugly words like that."

"I'll go make the lightning toilet, Henrietta. Do run like a good girl and ask Mrs. Hargrove to let Cousin Jasmine have her cup of coffee right away. I'll be there before the rest are dead from hunger," and Cousin James skilfully interrupted the threatened feminine clash as he emptied my glass bowl into his tin can and stuck the sharp stick in the ground for future reference. Even Henrietta's pointed allusion to his toilet had not in the least ruffled his equanimity or brought a shade of consciousness to his face.

"Mis' Hargrove said that the Bible said not for any woman to say a blessing at any table or at any place that anybody can hear her, when Cousin Marfy wanted to be polite to the Lord by saying just a little one and go on before we was all too hungry," answered Henrietta, in her most scornfully tolerant voice. "If women eat out loud before everybody why can't they pray their thank-you out loud like any man?"

"Answer her, Evelina," laughed Cousin James, as he hurried down the walk away from us.

"Henrietta," I asked, in a calmly argumentative tone of voice as she and I walked up the path to the house, "didn't Mr. Haley talk to you just yesterday and tell you how wicked it is for you to use - use such strong words as you do?"

Mr. Haley had told me just a few days ago that he and Aunt Augusta had agreed to open their campaign of reform on Henrietta by a pastoral lecture from him, to be followed strongly by a neighborly one from her.

"No, he never did any such thing," answered Henrietta, promptly - and what Henrietta says is always the truth, because she isn't afraid of anybody or anything enough to tell a lie - "he just telled me over and over in a whole lot of words how I ought to love and be good to Sallie. If I was to love Sallie that kind of way, he said, I would be so busy I couldn't do none of the things Sallie don't like to do herself and makes me do. 'Stid er saying, 'my precious mother, I love you and want to be good because you want me to,' about every hour, I had better wipe the twins' noses, and wash the dirt often them, and light Aunt Dilsie's phthisic pipe, and get things upstairs for Sallie and Miss Jasmine and everybody when they are downstairs. I'm too busy, I am, to be so religious. And I'm too hungry to talk any more about it." With which she departed.

I sank on the side steps and laughed until a busy old bumble-bee came down from a late honeysuckle blossom and buzzed around to see what it was all about. Henrietta's statement of the case was a graphic and just one. Sallie has got a tendril around Henrietta which grows by the day. Poor tot, she does have a hard and hardening time - and how can I lecture her for swearing?

With a train of thought started by Henrietta I sat at my solitary breakfast in a deeply contemplative mood. Life was going to press hard on Henrietta. And reared in the fossilized atmosphere of Widegables, which tried to draw all its six separate feminine breaths as one with a lone, supporting man, how was she to develop the biceps of strength of mind and soul, as well as body, to meet the conditions she was likely to have to meet? Still her coming tussle with Aunt Augusta would be a tonic at least. I was just breaking a last muffin and beginning to smile when I saw a delegation coming down the street and turning into my front gate; I rose to meet it with distinction.

Aunt Augusta marched at the head and Nell and Caroline were on each side of her, while Sallie and Mamie Hall brought up the rear, walking more deliberately and each carrying a baby, comparing some sort of white tags of sewing. Cousin Martha was crossing the Road in their wake with her knitting bag and palm leaf fan.

One thing I am proud of having accomplished this summer is the establishing of friendly relations with Aunt Augusta. I made up my mind that she probably needed to have some of my affection ladled out to her more than anybody in Glendale, and I worked on all the volatile fear and resentment and dislike I had ever had for her all my life, and I have succeeded in liquefying it into a genuine liking for the martial old personality. If Aunt Augusta had been a man she would have probably led a regiment up San Juan Hill, died in the trenches, and covered herself and family with glory. She is the newest woman in the Harpeth Valley, and though sixty years old, she is lineally Sallie Carruthers's own granddaughter.

"Evelina," she began, as soon as she had martialed her forces into rocking-chairs, though she had Jasper bring her the stiffest and straightest-backed one in the house, "I have collected as many women as I had time to, and have come up here to tell you, and them, that the men in Glendale are so lacking in sense and judgment that the time has come for women to stand forth and assume the responsibility of them and Glendale in general. As the wife of the poor decrepit Mayor, I appoint myself chairman of the meeting pro tem and ask you to take the first minutes. If disgrace is threatening us we must at least

Maria Thompson Daviess

face it in an orderly and parliamentary way. And I - "

"Oh, Mrs. Shelby, is it - is it smallpox?" and as Sallie spoke she hugged up the Puppy baby, who happened to be the twin in her arms, so that she bubbled and giggled, mistaking her embraces for those of frolicsome affection.

Mamie turned pale and held her baby tight and I could see that she was having light spasms of alarm, one for each one of the children and one for Ned.

"Smallpox, fiddlesticks - I said disgrace, Sallie Carruthers, and the worst kind of disgrace - municipal disgrace." And as Aunt Augusta named the plague that was to come upon us, she looked as if she expected it to wilt us all into sear and dried leaves. And in point of fact, we all did rustle.

"Tell us about it," said Nell, with sparkling eyes and sitting up in her low rocker as straight as Aunt Augusta did in her uncompromising seat. The rest of them just looked helpless and undecided as to whether to be relieved or not.

"Yes, municipal disgrace threatens the town, and the women must rise in their strength and avert it," she declaimed majestically with her dark eyes snapping.

"Yesterday afternoon James Hardin, who is the only patriotic male in Glendale, put before the Town Council a most reasonable and pride-bestirring proposition originated by Evelina Shelby, one of Glendale's leading citizens, though a woman. She wants to offer the far-famed hospitality of Glendale - which is the oldest and most aristocratic town in the Harpeth Valley, except perhaps Hillsboro, and which is not in the class with a vulgarly rich, modern place like Bolivar, that has a soap-factory and streetcars, and was a mud-hole in the landscape when the first Shelby built this very house, - to the Commission of magnates who are to come down about the railroad lines that are to be laid near us. James agrees with her and urges that it is fitting and dignified that, when they are through with their vulgar trafficking over at insignificant Bolivar, they be asked to partake of real southern hospitality at its fountain head, especially as Evelina is obliged to invite two of them as personal friends. Do you not see it in that light?" And Aunt Augusta looked at us with the martial mien of a general commanding his army for a campaign.

"It would be nice," answered Mamie, as she turned little Ned over on his stomach across her knee and began to sway him and trot him at the same time, which was his signal to get off into a nap. "But Ned said last night that he had lost so much in the bond subscription, that he didn't feel like spending any more money for an entertainment, that wouldn't do one bit of good about the taxes or bonds or anything. The baby was beginning to fret, so I don't think I understood it exactly."

"I don't think you did," answered Aunt Augusta, witheringly, "That is not the point at all, and - "

"But Mr. Greenfield said last night, while he was discussing it with Father, that it would do no good whatever and probably be an embarrassment to the Commission, our putting in a pitiful bid like that. He - " but Caroline got no further with the feminine echo of her masculine opinion-former.

"Peter Shelby put that objection much more picturesquely than Lee Greenfield," Aunt Augusta snapped. "He said that licking those men's hands would turn his stomach, after swallowing that bond issue. However, all this has nothing to do with the case. I am trying to - "

"Polk said last night that he thought it would be much more spectacular for all the good looking women in town to go when we are invited to Mrs. Henderson's tea for the big bugs, and dazzle 'em so that it would at least put Glendale on the map," said Nell, with spirit. "He made me so mad that I - "

"Mr. Haley thinks that we should be very careful not to feel malice or envy towards Bolivar, but to rejoice at their good fortune in getting both roads and the shops, even if it does mean a loss to us. What is material wealth in this world anyway when we can depend so on - "Sallie's expression was so beautifully silly and like the Dominie's, that it was all that I could do not to give vent to an unworthy shout. Nell saw it as I did and I felt her smother a giggle.

But before Aunt Augusta could get her breath to put the crux of the matter straight before her feminine tribunal, Aunt Martha beat her to it as she placidly rocked back and forth knitting lace for a petticoat for Henrietta.

"Of course, Glendale doesn't really care about the railroad; in fact, we would much rather not have our seclusion broken in upon, especially as they might choose the route they have prospected" - with a glance at Sallie - "but it is to show them our friendliness, more Bolivar than the actual Commission, and our desire to rejoice with them in their good fortune. It would be very mean spirited of us to ignore them and not assist them in entertaining their guests, especially as some of them must be invited. We've never been in such an attitude as that to Bolivar!"

"Exactly, Martha," answered Aunt Augusta with relief. "The thought of proud old Glendale putting herself in an attitude of municipal sulks towards common Bolivar seemed an unbearable disgrace to me. Didn't we invite them up for a great fish-fry on the river when they opened that odious soap factory, and ask them to let us help take care of some of their delegates when they had the Methodist Conference? They sent one of the two bishops to you, you remember, Martha, and I am sure your entertainment of him was so lavish that he went home ill. No man said us nay in the exercising our right of religious hospitality, why should they in our civic? We must not allow the town to put us in such an attitude! Must Not! It was for this that I called this meeting at Evelina's, as she was the one to propose this public-spirited and creditable plan."

"But what shall we do if they don't want to have it?" asked Mamie.

"I have asked, when did the men of Glendale begin to dictate to the women as to whom they should offer their hospitality?" answered Aunt Augusta, as she arose to her feet. "Are we free women, and have we, or have we not, command of our own storerooms and our own servants and our own time and strength?"

And as I looked up at the tall, fierce, white-haired old dame of high degree, daughter of the women of the Colonies and the women of the Wilderness days, I got exactly the same sensation I had when I saw the Goddess of Liberty loom up out of the mist as I sailed into the harbor of my own land from a foreign one. And what I was feeling I knew every woman present was feeling in a greater or less degree, except perhaps Sallie, for her face was a puzzle of sore amazement and a pleading desire for further sleep.

"Have we or have we not?" Aunt Augusta again

Maria Thompson Daviess

demanded, and just then a most wonderful thing happened!

Jane stood in our midst!

Oh, Jane, you were a miracle to me, but I must go on writing about it all calmly for the sake of the Five!

I made a mad rush from my rocker to throw myself into her arms, but she stopped me with one glance of her cold, official eye that quelled me, and stood attention before Aunt Augusta.

"Madam President," she said in her grandest parliamentary voice, "it was by accident that I interrupted the proceedings of what I take to be an official meeting. Have I your permission to withdraw? I am Miss Shelby's guest, Miss Mathers, and I can easily await her greetings until the adjournment of this body."

Oh, Jane, and my arms just hungry for you!

"Madam," answered Aunt Augusta, in her grandest manner and a voice so filled with cordiality that I hardly knew it, "it is the pleasure of the chair to interrupt proceedings and to welcome you. Evelina, introduce us all!"

It was all just glorious! I never saw anybody get a more lovely ovation than Jane did from my friends, for they had all heard about her, read with awe clippings I showed them about her speeches and - were about ready for her.

Sallie kissed her on both cheeks, Mamie laid the baby in her arms with a devout expression, and Nell clung to her with the rapture of the newly proselyted in her face. Aunt Martha made her welcome in her dearest manner and

Caroline beamed on her with the return of a lot of the fire and spirit of the youth that hanging on the doled-out affections of Lee Greenfield had starved in her.

And it was characteristic of Jane and her methods that it took much less time than it takes me to write it, for her to get all the greetings over with, explain that she had sent me a letter telling me that she was coming that must have gone astray, get everybody named and ticketed in her mind, and get us all back to business.

Aunt Augusta explained the situation to her with so much feeling and eloquence that she swept us all off our feet, and when she was ready to put the question again to us as to our willingness to embark on our defiance of our fellow-townsmen, the answer of enthusiastic acquiescence was ready for her.

"Of course, as none of you have any official municipal status, the invitation will have to be given informally, in a social way, to the Commission through Miss Shelby's friend, Mr. Richard Hall," said Jane, when Aunt Augusta had called on her to give us her opinion of the situation in general and the mode of procedure. "We find it best in all women-questions of the present, to do things in a perfectly legal and parliamentary way."

"Must we tell them about it or not?" asked Mamie, in a wavering voice, looking up devoutly at Jane, who had held young Ned against the stiff white linen shirt of her traveling dress just as comfortably as if he were her own seventh.

"Did they consult you before deciding to refuse your suggestion?" asked Jane, calmly and thoughtfully.

"They did not," trumpeted Aunt Augusta.

"Then wouldn't it be the most regular way to proceed to get an acceptance of the invitation from the Commission and then extend them one to be present?" pronounced Jane, coolly, seemingly totally unconscious that she was exploding; a bomb shell.

"It would, and we will consider it so settled," answered Aunt Augusta, dominatingly.

This quick and revolutionary decision gave me a shock. I could see that a woman doesn't like to feel that there is a stick of dynamite between her and a man, when she puts her head down under his chin or her cheek to his, but advanced women must suffer that. Still I'm glad that the Crag is on our side of the fence. I felt sorry for Mamie and Caroline - and Sallie looked a tragedy.

In fact, a shade of depression was about to steal over the spirits of the meeting when Aunt Augusta luckily called for the discussion of plans for the rally.

Feeding other human beings is the natural, instituted, physiological, pathological, metaphysical, and spiritual outlet for a woman's nature, and that is why she is so happy when she gets out her family receipt book for a called rehearsal for the functioning of her hospitality. The revolution went home happy and excited over the martialing of their flesh pots.

I'm glad Jane is asleep across the hall to-night. If I had had to shoulder all this outbreak by myself I would have compromised by instituting a campaign of wheedling, the like of which this town never suffered before, and then when this glorious rally was finally pulled off, the cajoled masculine population would have fairly swelled with pride over having done it!

Of course, by every known test of conduct and economics, their attitude in the matter is entirely right. Men work to all given points in straight, clear-cut, logical lines only to find women at the point of results waiting for them, with unforeseen culminations, which would have been impossible to them.

And I am also glad the Crag is partly responsible for starting, or at least unconsciously aiding, this scheme in high finance of mine; and he is also in reality the silent sponsor for this unhatched revolution. I am deeply contented to go to sleep with that comforting; thought tucked under my pillow.

CHAPTER VIII

AN ATTAINED TO-MORROW

I've changed my mind about a woman's being like a whirlwind. The women of now are the attained to-morrow that the world since the beginning has been trying to catch up with. Jane is that, and then the day after, too, and what she has done to Glendale in these two weeks has stunned the old town into a trance of delight and amazement. She has recreated us, breathed the breath of modernity into us, and started the machine up the grade of civilization at a pace that makes me hold my breath for fear of something jolting us.

She and Aunt Augusta have organized an Equality League, and that wheel came very near flying loose and being the finish of Uncle Peter.

He came to see me the morning of the first meeting and, when I saw him coming up the front walk, I got an astral vision of the chips on his shoulder enlarged to twice their natural size, and called to Jasper to mix the juleps very long and extra deep. But deep as they were, to the very top of the longest glasses, he couldn't drown his wrath in his.

"Women, women," he exploded from over the very mint sprig itself, "all fools, all fools from the beginning of time; made that way on purpose - on purpose - hey?

World needs some sort of creature with no better sense than to want to spend their lives fooling with babies and the bread of life. Human young and religion are the only things in the world men can't attend to for themselves and that's what they need women for. Women with no brains - but all heart - all heart - hey?"

"Why should just a little brain hurt their heart-action. Uncle Peter?" I asked mildly. There is nothing in the world that I ever met that I enjoy any more than one of Uncle Peter's rages, and I always try to be meekly inflammatory.

"They're never satisfied with using them to run church societies and children's internal organs, but they want to use 'em on men and civilization in general. Where'd you get that Yankee school-marm - hey? Why don't she get a husband and a baby and settle down? Ten babies, twenty babies if necessary - hey?"

"You are entirely mistaken as to the plans that Jane and Aunt Augusta have for the League they are forming this morning, Uncle Peter." I began to say with delight as to what was likely to ensue. "If you would only listen to Jane while she - "

"Don't want to hear a word she has to say! All 'as the crackling of thorns under a pot' - all the talk of fools."

"But surely you are not afraid to listen to her, Uncle Peter," I dared to say, and then stood away.

"Afraid, afraid - never was afraid of anybody in my life, Augusta not excepted!" he exclaimed, as he rose in his wrath. "The men of this town will show the uprising hussies what we think of 'em, and put 'em back to the heels of men, where they belong - belong - hey?"

And before I could remonstrate with him he was marching down the street like a whole regiment out on a charge that was to be one of extermination, or complete surrender.

The Crag told me that evening that the Mayor's office of Glendale had reeked of brimstone, for hours, and the next Sunday Aunt Augusta sat in their pew at church, militantly alone, while he occupied a seat in the farthest limits of the amen corner, with equal militancy.

But Uncle Peter's attitude during the time of Jane's campaign for general Equality in Glendale was pathetically like that of an old log, that has been drifting comfortably down the stream of life with the tide that bore its comrades, and suddenly got its end stuck in the mud so that it was forced to stem alone the very tide it had been floating on.

Jane didn't throw any rocks at anybody's opinions or break the windows of anybody's prejudices. She had the most lovely heart to heart talks with the women separately, collectively, and in both small and large bunches. I had them in to tea in the combinations that she wanted them, and I must say that she was the loveliest thing with them that could be imagined. She was just her stiff, ugly self, starchily clad in the most beautifully tailored white linen, and they all went mad about her. The Pup and the Kit clutched at her skirts until anybody else would have been a mass of wrinkles, and the left breast of her linen blouse did always bear a slight impress of little Ned's head. The congeniality of Jane and that baby was a revelation to me and his colic ceased after the first time she kneaded it out of his fat little stomach with her long, slim, powerful hands according to a first-aid method she had learned in her settlement work, with Mamie looking on in fear and adoration. It may have been bloodless surgery but I suspect it of being partly hypnotism, because the same sort of surgery was used on the minds of all my women friends and with a like result.

The subject of the rally was a fine one for everybody to get together on from the start and, before any of them realized that they were doing anything but plan out the details of a big spread, the like of which they had been doing for hospitable generations, for the railroad Commission, they were organized into a flourishing Equality League, with officers and by-laws and a sinking fund in the treasury.

"Now, Evelina," said Jane, as she sat on the edge of my bed braiding her heavy, sleek, black braid that is as big as my wrist and that she declares is her one beauty, though she ought to know that her straight, strong-figure, ruddy complexion, aroma of strength and keen, near-sighted eyes are - well, if not beauties, something very winning, "we must not allow the men time to get sore over this matter of the League. We must make them feel immediately that they are needed and wanted intensely in the movement. They must be asked to take their place, shoulder to shoulder, with us in this fight for better conditions for the world and mankind in general. True to our theory we must offer them our comradely affection and openly and honestly express our need of them in our lives and in our activities. I was talking to Mrs. Carruthers and Nell and Mrs. Hall and Caroline, as well as your Cousin Martha, about it this afternoon and they all agreed with me that the men would have cause to be aggrieved at us about seeming thus to be organizing a life for ourselves apart from theirs, with no place in it provided for them. Mrs. Carruthers said that she had felt that the Reverend Mr. Haley had been deeply hurt already at not being masked to open any of the meetings with prayer, and she volunteered to talk to him and express for herself and us our need of him."

"That will be easy for Sallie, for she has been expressing need of people in her fife as long as she has been living it," I answered with a good-natured laugh, though I would have liked to have that interview with the Dominie myself. He is so enthusiastic that I like to bask in him once in a while.

"I asked young Mr. Hayes to take me fishing with him tomorrow in order to have a whole quiet day with him alone so that we could get closely in touch with each other. I have had very little opportunity to talk with him, but I have felt his sympathy in several interested glances we have exchanged with each other. I am looking forward to the establishment of a perfect friendship with him."

I told myself that I was mistaken in thinking that the expression in Jane's eyes was softened to the verge of dreaminess and my inmost soul shouted at the idea of Jane and Polk and their day alone in the woods.

Since that night that Polk humiliated me as completely as a man can humiliate a woman, he has looked at me like a whipped child, and I haven't looked at him at all I have used Jane as a wide-spread fan behind which to hide from him. How was I to know what was going on on the other side of the fan?

It is a relief to realize that in the world there are at least a few women like Jane that don't have to be protected from Polk and his kind. Jane is one of the hunted that has turned and has come back to meet the pursuer with outstretched and disarming hand. This, I suspect, is to be about her first real tussle; skoal to the victor!

"I advised your Aunt Augusta to ask you to talk again to

your Uncle Peter, and Nell is to seek an interview with Mr. Hardin at her earliest opportunity, though I think the only result will be instruction and uplift for Nell, as a more illumined thing I never had said to me on the subject of the relation of men and women than the one he uttered to me last night, as he said good-by to me out on the porch in that glorious moonlight that seems brighter here in Glendale than I have ever seen it out in the world anywhere else."

"What did he say?" I asked perfectly naturally, though a double-bladed pain was twisted around in my solar plexus as the vision of Jane's last night interview in the moonlight with the Crag, and Nell's soon-to-be-one, hit me broadside at the same time. I haven't had one by myself with him for a week.

"Why, of course, women are the breath that men draw into their lungs of life to supply eternal combustion," was what he said when I asked him point-blank what he thought of the League. "Only let us breathe slowly as we ascend to still greater elevations with their consequent rarefied air," he added, with the most heavenly thoughtfulness in his fine face. "Did it ever occur to you, Evelina, that your Cousin James is really a radiantly beautiful man? How could you be so mistaken, as to both him and his personal appearance, as to apply such a name as Crag to him?"

Glendale is going to Jane's head!

"Don't you think he looks scraggy in that long-tailed coat, shocks of taggy hair and a collar big enough to fit Old Harpeth?" I asked deceitfully.

Why shouldn't I tell Jane what I really thought of Cousin James and discuss him broadly and frankly? I don't know!

Lately I don't want to think about him or have anybody mention him in my presence. I've got a consciousness of him way off in a corner of me somewhere and I'm just brooding over it. Everybody in town has been in this house since Jane has been here, all the time, and I haven't seen him alone for ages it seems. Maybe that's why I have had to make a desert island inside myself to take him to.

"And I have been thinking since you told me of the situation in which he and Mrs. Carruthers have been placed by this financial catastrophe, how wonderful it will be if love really does come to them, when her grief is healed by time. He will rear her interesting children into women that will be invaluable to the commonwealth," Jane continued as she tied a blue bow on the end of her long black plait.

"Do you think that there - there are any signs of - of such a thing yet?" I asked with pitiful weakness as I wilted down into my pillow.

"Just a bit in his manner to her, though I may be influenced in my judgment by the evident suitability of such a solution of the situation," she answered as she settled herself back against one of the posts of my high old bed and looked me clean through and through, even unto the shores of that desert island itself.

"I hope you have been noting these different emotional situations and reactions among your friends carefully in your record, Evelina," she continued in an interested and biological tone of voice and expression of eye. "In a small community like this it is much easier to get at the real underlying motive of such things than it is in a more complicated civilization. I have seen you transcribing notes into our book. Since I have come to Glendale I am more firmly determined than ever that the attitude of emotional equality that we determined upon in the spring is the true solution of most of the complicated man-and-woman problems. I am anxious to see it tried out in five other different communities that we will select. I would not seem to be indelicate, dear, but I do not see any signs of your having been especially drawn emotionally towards any of your friends, though your attitude of sisterly comradeship and frankness with them is more beautiful than I thought it was possible for such a thing to be. You are not being tempted to shirk any of your duties of womanhood because of your interest in your art, are you? I will confess to you that the thing that brought me down upon you was your news of this commission for the series of station-gardens. I think you will probably work better after this side of your nature is at rest. Of course, a union with Mr. Hall would be ideal for you. You must consider it seriously."

The "must" in Jane's voice sounded exactly like that "must" looked in Richard's telegram, which has been enforced with others just as emphatic ever since.

There are some men who are big enough to take a woman with a wound in her heart and heal both it and her by their love. Richard is one of that kind. What could any woman want more than her work and a man like that?

After Jane had laid her strong-minded head on the hard pillow, that I had had to have concocted out of bats of cotton for her, I laid my face against my own made of the soft breast feathers of a white flock of hovering hen-mothers and wept on their softness.

A light was burning down in the lodge at the gate of Widegables. He hasn't gone back to his room to sleep, even when I have Jane's strong-mindedness in the house with me. I remember that I gave my word of honor to myself that I wouldn't try any of my modern emotional experiments on him the first night I slept in this house alone, with only him over there to keep me from dying with primitive woman fright. I shall keep my word to myself and propose to Richard if my contract with Jane and the Five seems to call for it. In the meantime if I choose to cry myself to sleep it is nobody's business.

I wonder if a mist rises up to Heaven every night from all the woman-tears in all the world, and if God sees it, as it clings damp around the hem of His garment, and smiles with such warm understanding that it vanishes in a soft glow of sleep that He sends down to us!

Jane has arisen early several mornings and spent an hour before breakfast composing a masterly and Machiavellian letter of invitation from the Equality League to the inhabitants of Glendale and the surrounding countryside to and beyond Bolivar to attend the rally given by them in honor of the C. & G. Railroad Commission on Tuesday next. It is to come out to-day in the weekly papers of Glendale, Bolivar, Hillsboro, and Providence, and I hope there will not be so many cases of heart-failure from rage that the gloom of many funerals will put out the light of the rally. I hope no man will beat any woman in the Harpeth Valley for it, and if he does, I hope he will do it so neither Jane nor I will hear of it.

It was Aunt Augusta who thought up the insulting and incendiary plan of having the rally as an offering of hospitality from the League, and I hope if Uncle Peter is going to die over it he will not have the final explosion in my presence.

Privately I spent a dollar and a half sending a night-letter to Richard all about it and asking him if the Commissioners would be willing to stand for this feminist plank in the barbecue deal. He had sent me the nicest letter of acceptance from the Board when I had written the invitation to them through him, as coming from the perfectly ladylike feminine population of Glendale, and I didn't like to get them into a woman-whirlwind without their own consent. I paid the boy at the telegraph office five dollars not to talk about the matter to a human soul, and threatened to have him dismissed if he did, so the bomb-shell was kept in until this afternoon.

Richard replied to the telegram with characteristic directness:

> Delighted to be in at the fight. Seven of us rabid suffragists, two on the fence, and a half roast pig will convert the other. Found no answer to my question in letter of last Tuesday. Must!
>
> RICHARD.

It was nice of Jane to write out and get ready her bomb-shell and then go off with Polk, so as not to see it explode. But I'm glad she did. However, I did advise her to take a copy of it along with the reels and the lunch-basket to read to him, as a starter of their day to be devoted to the establishment of a perfect friendship between them.

Polk didn't look at me even once as I helped pack them and their traps into his Hupp, but Solomon in all his glory was not arrayed like Polk in his white flannels, and he and Jane made a picture of perfectly blended tailored smartness as they got ready for the break-away.

There are some men that acquire feminine obligations as rough cheviot does lint and Henrietta is one of Polk's when it comes to the fishing days. He takes her so often that she thinks she owns him and all the trout in Little

Harpeth, and she landed in the midst of the picnic with her fighting clothes on.

"Where are you and her going at, - fishing?" she asked in a calmly controlled voice that both of them had heard before, and which made us quail in our boots and metaphorically duck our heads.

"Yes, we - er thought we would," he answered with an uncertainty of voice and manner that bespoke abject fear.

"I'll be d - if you shall," came the explosion, hot and loud. "I want to go fishing with you, Polk, my own self, and she ain't no good for nothing any way. You can't take her!"

"Henrietta!" I both beseeched and commanded in one breath.

"No, she ain't no good at all," was reiterated in the stormy young voice as Henrietta caught hold of the nose of the panting Hupp and stooddirectly in the path of destruction, if Polk had turned the driving wheel a hair's breadth. "Uncle Peter says that she is er going to turn the devil loose in Glendale, so they won't be no more whisky and no more babies borned and men will get they noses rubbed in their plates, if they don't eat the awful truck she is er going to teach the women to cook for their husbands. An' the men won't marry no more then at all, and I'll have to be a old maid like her."

Now, why did I write weeks ago that I would like to witness an encounter between Jane and Henrietta! I didn't mean it, but I got it!

Without ruffling a hair or changing color Jane stepped out of the Hupp and faced the foe. Henrietta is a tiny scrap of a woman, intense in a wild, beautiful, almost hunted kind of way, and she is so thin that it makes my heart ache. She is being fairly crushed with the beautiful depending weight of her mother and the responsibility of the twins, and somehow she is most pathetic. I made a motion to step between her and Jane, but one look in Jane's face stopped me.

"Dear," she said, in her rich, throaty, strong voice as she looked pleadingly at the militant midget facing her. Suddenly I was that lonesome, homesick freshman by the waters of Lake Waban, with Jane's awkward young arm around me, and I stood aside to let Henrietta come into her heritage of Jane. "Don't you want to come with us?" was the soft question that followed the commanding word of endearment.

"No!" was the short, but slightly mollified answer as Henrietta dug her toes into the dust and began to look fascinated.

"I'm glad you don't want to come, because I've got some very important business to ask you to attend to for me," answered Jane, in the brisk tone of voice she uses in doing business with women, and which interests them intensely by its very novelty and flatters them by seeming to endow them with a kind of brain they didn't know they possessed. "I want you to go upstairs and get my pocketbook. Be careful, for there is over a hundred dollars in the roll of bills - Evelina will give you the key to the desk - and go down to the drug store where they keep nice little clocks and buy me the best one they have. Then please you wind it up yourself and watch it all day to see if it keeps time with the clock in your hall, and if it varies more than one minute, take it back and get another. While you are in the drug store, if you have time, won't you please select me a new tooth-brush and some nice kind of paste that you think is good? Make them show you all they have. Pay for it out of one of the bills."

"Want any good, smelly soap?" I came out of my trance of absolute admiration to hear Henrietta ask in the capable voice of a secretary to a millionaire. Her thin little face was flushed with excitement and importance, and she edged two feet nearer the charmer.

"It would be a good thing to get about a half dozen cakes, wouldn't it?" answered Jane, with slight uncertainty in her voice as if leaving the decision of the matter partly to Henrietta.

"Yes, I believe I would," Henrietta decided judicially. "The 'New Mown Hay' is what Jasper got for Petunia because he hit her too hard last week and swelled her eye. They is a perfumery that goes with it at one quarter a bottle. That makes it all cheaper."

"Exactly the thing, and we mustn't spend money unnecessarily," Jane agreed. "But I don't want to trespass on your time, Henrietta, dear," she added with the deference she would have used in speaking to the President of the Nation League or the founder of Hull House.

"No, ma'am, I'm glad to do it, and I'll go quick 'fore it gets any later in the day for me to watch the clock," answered Henrietta in stately tones that were very like Jane's and which I had never heard her employ before.

And before any of the three of us got our breath her bare little feet were flashing up my front walk.

"Help!" exclaimed Polk as he leaned back from his wheel and fanned himself with his hat. "Do you use the same methods with grown beasts that you do with cubs?" he added weakly.

"It's the same she has always used on me, only this is more dramatic. Beware!" I said with a laugh as I insisted on just one squeeze of Jane's white linen arm as she was climbing back into the car.

"That's a remarkably fine child and she should have good, dependable, business-like habits put in the place of faulty and useless ones. Her profanity will make no difference for the present and can be easily corrected. Don't interfere with her attending to my commissions, Evelina. Let's start, Mr. Hayes." And Jane settled herself calmly for the spin out Providence Road.

"All the hundred dollars all by herself, Jane?" I called after them.

"Yes," floated back positively in the wake of the Hupp.

For several hours I attended to the business of my life in a haze of meditation. If Henrietta ticks off the same number of minutes on the woman-clock from Jane's standpoint, that Jane has marked off from her own mother's, high noon is going to strike before we are ready for it.

But it was only an hour or two of high-minded communing with the future that I got the time for, before I was involved in the whirl of dust that swirled around the storm center, to darken and throw a shadow over Glendale about the time of the publication of the Glendale News, which occurs every Thursday near the hour of noon, so that all the subscribers can take that enterprising sheet home to consume while waiting for dinner, and can leave it for the women of their families to enjoy in the afternoon.

I suspect that the digestion of Jane's Equality rally

invitation interfered with the digestion of much fried chicken, corn, and sweet potatoes, under the roof-trees of the town and I spent the afternoon in hearing results and keeping up the spirits of the insurgents.

Caroline came in with her head so high that she had difficulty in seeing over her very slender and aristocratic nose, with a note from Lee Greenfield which had just come to her, asking her to go with him in his car over to Hillsboro to spend the day with Tom Pollard's wife, a visit he knows she has been dying to make for two months, for she was one of Pet's bridesmaids. He made casual and dastardly mention that there would be a moon to come home by, but ignored completely the fact that Tuesday was the day on which he had been invited by the League, of which he knew she was a member, to meet and rally around the C. & G. Commission.

I helped her compose the answer, and I must say we hit Lee only in high spots. I could see she was scared to death, and so was I, but her dander was up, and I backed mine up along side it for the purpose of support. Besides I feel in my heart that that note will dynamite the rocky old situation between them into something more easily handled.

She had just gone to dispatch the missive by their negro gardener when Mamie and Sallie came clucking in. Mamie's face was pink and high-spirited, but Sallie was in one complete slump of mind and body.

"Mr. Haley has just stopped by to say that he thinks no price is too great to pay for peace, and fellowship, and good-will in a community," she said, as she dropped into a rocker and looked pensively after the retreating figure of the handsome young Dominie, who had accompanied them to the gate but wisely no farther. He didn't know that

Jane had gone with Polk.

"And women to pay the price," answered Mamie, spiritedly. "I have just told Ned that as yet I do not know enough to argue the question of woman's wrongs with him, but I have learned a few of her rights. One of *mine* is to have him accept any invitation I am responsible for having my friends offer him, and to accompany me to the entertainment if I desire to go. I reminded him that I had not troubled him often as an escort since my marriage. He was so scared that he almost let little Ned drop out of his arms, and he got in an awful hurry to go to town, but he asked me to have his gray flannels pressed before Tuesday and to buy him a blue tie to go with a new shirt he has. I never like to spank Ned or the children, but I must say it does clear the atmosphere."

"You don't think we could put it off or - or - " Sallie faltered.

"No!" answered Mamie and I together, and as I spoke I called Jasper to set out more rockers and have Petunia get the tea-tray ready, for I saw Aunt Augusta go across the road to collect Cousin Martha and Mrs. Hargrove and the rest, while Nell whirled by in her rakish little car on her way to the Square and called that she would be back.

When Nell used a thousand dollars of her own money, left her by her grandmother, to buy that little Buick, Glendale promptly had a spell of epilepsy that lasted for days. The whole town still dodges and swears when it sees her coming, for she drives with a combination of feminine recklessness and masculine speed that is to say the least alarming. To see Aunt Augusta out for a spin with her is a delicious sight.

And it was most interesting to listen to a minute

description of the composite fit thrown by the male population of Glendale, at their rally invitation, but as time was limited I finally coaxed the conversation around to the subject of the viands to be offered the lordly creatures in the way of propitiation for the insult that we were forcing them to swallow by taking matters in our own hands, and then we had a really glorious time.

I am glad I have had a year or more in Paris, months in Italy, weeks in Berlin, and a sojourn in England, just so that I can be sure myself and assure the others with authority that there are no such cooks in all the world as the women in the Harpeth Valley of Tennessee, United States of America.

The afternoon wore away on the wings of magic, and the long, purple shadows were falling across the street, a rustle of cool night wind was stirring the tree-tops and the first star was coming timidly out into the gloaming, before they all realized that it was time to hurry and scurry under roof-trees.

Lee Greenfield was waiting at the gate for Caroline.

Just as Henrietta had taken a last peep at the clock on the hall table and gone to answer Sallie's call to come and help Aunt Dilsie in the bedding of the Kitten and the Pup, Polk's Hupp stopped at the gate, and he and Jane came up the front walk in the twilight together.

She had on his flannel coat over her linen one and his expression was one of glorified and translucent daze. I didn't look at her - I felt as if I couldn't. I was scared! For a second she held me in her arms and kissed me, *really* - the first time she had ever done it in all my life - and then went on upstairs with a nice, cool good-night and "thank you" to Polk.

"Evelina," he said, as he handed me the empty lunch-basket and also the empty fish-bucket, the first he had ever in his life brought in from Little Harpeth, "I was right about that Hallelujah chorus being the true definition of the real woman - only they are more so. I have seen a light, and you pointed the way. Will you forgive me for being what I was - and trust me - with - with - good-night!" He was gone!

Jane's kiss had been one of revelation - to me!

For a long time I sat out there in the cool, hazy, windy autumn twilight breeze, that was heavy with the scent of luscious wild grapes and tasseled corn, fanning the flame of loneliness in me until I couldn't have stood it any longer if a tall gray figure of relief had not come up the street and called me down to my front gate.

"Hail the instigator of a bloodless revolution," laughed the Crag as I stopped myself with difficulty on the opposite side of the gate from him. "The city fathers will have to capitulate, and now for the reign of the mothers!"

"And the same old route to subjection chosen, through their stomachs to their civic hearts," I answered impudently.

Overlooking my pertness he went on:

"Mayor Shelby was at home with Mrs. Augusta for two hours after dinner and, as I came by the post-office, I heard him telling Polk in remarkably chastened, if not entirely chaste language, that it was 'better to let the women have their kick-up on a feeding proposition than on something worse,' as he classically put it."

"I know it is a great victory," I answered weakly, "but I'm

too tired to glory in it. I wish I was Sallie's Puppy being trotted across Aunt Dilsie's knee, or Kit, getting a rocking in Cousin Martha's arms."

"Would any other arms do for the rocking?" came in a queer, audacious voice, with a note in it that stilled something in me and made all the world seem to be holding its breath.

"I'm tired of revoluting and it's - it's tenderness I want," I faltered in a voice that hardly seemed strong enough to get so far up out of my heart as to reach the ears of the Crag as he bent his head down close over mine. He had come on my side of the gate at the first weak little cry I had let myself make a minute or two before.

"Is this right?" he asked, as he gently took me in his arms, hollowed his shoulder for a place for my head, and leaning against the old gate he began to swing me gently to and fro, his cheek aga inst my hairand humming Aunt Dilsie's

"Swing low sweet chariot, fer to carry me home."

It was.

I know now what I want and I am going to have it. I'll fight the whole world with naked hands for him. And I'm also going to find some way to get him with all his absurd niceties of honor intact, just because that will make him happier.

I'll begin at the beginning and some way unclasp those gourdy tendrils that Sallie has been strangling him with. I will bunch all the rest of his feminine collection and take them on my own hands. I'm going to make a Governor out of him, and then a United States Senator and finally a

Supreme Judge. Help! Think of the old Mossback being a progressive, but that's my party and Jane's.

I know he is going to hate terribly to have me ask him to marry me, and I hate to hurt him so, but it is my duty to get Jane's fifty thousand dollars so the Five may be as happy as I am to-night; only there aren't five other Crags. I know it will be a life-long mortification to him to have me do it, but he lost his chance to-night grand-mothering me. Still, I did turn my lips away. I was not quite ready then - I am now.

If he wants to go on wearing clothes like that I'm going to let him, even on the Senate floor, but I can't ever stand for Cousin Jasmine to cut his hair any more. I want to do it myself, and I'm going to tell her so, and why. She and I have cried over that miniature of the lost young Confederate cousin of hers and she'll understand me.

But as I think it over - it always is best to be kind, and I believe I'll let him get through this rally - it's just four days - free and happy man.

I don't know whether to go in and wake up Jane or not. I would like to go to sleep with that kiss revelation between us, but maybe it is my duty to the Five to extract some data from her while it is fresh, on the foam. I am afraid it is going to go hard with her, but somehow I have a newborn faith in Polk that makes me feel that he will make it as easy as he can for her.

Isn't it a glorious thing to realize that neither she nor I will have to sit and be tortured by waiting to see what those men are going to do?

Maria Thompson Daviess

CHAPTER IX

DYNAMITE

When a man injures a woman's feelings by any particular course of conduct to which she objects, the maternal in her rises to the surface and she treats and forgives him as she would a naughty child, - but a man makes any kind of woman-affront into a lover's quarrel. That is what masculine Glendale has been doing to its women folks for four days, and I believe everybody has been secretly enjoying it.

As to the rally, they have stood aside with their hands in their pockets and their noses in the air, and if it hadn't been for Aunt Augusta and Nell and Jane being natural-born carpenters and draymen, we might have had to give it up and let them go on with it to their own glory.

When Nell and Jane went to see Mr. Dodd about building the long tables to serve the barbecue dinner on, he said he was too busy to do it and hadn't even any lumber to sell.

Then things happened in my back yard that it sounds like a romance to write about. Jane sent me over to borrow the Crag's team and wagon and Henrietta and Cousin Martha and any of the rest of his woman-impedimenta that I could get. He was out of town, trying a case over at Bolivar, and wouldn't get back until Monday night.

I am glad he wasn't here, for it would have gone hard with me to treat him in the manner that Jane decided it was best for all the women in Glendale to treat all the men in this crisis. It sounded sweet and cold as molasses dispenses itself to you in midwinter, and I could see it was a strain on Mamie and Caroline and Mrs. Kirkland, Nell's mother, and young Mrs. Dodd, the carpenter's wife, - the Boston girl that married him before she realized him, - to keep it up from day to day.

Besides that I'm going to be a politician's wife - though he doesn't know it yet - and I want the Crag to be away from the necessity of taking any sides in this civilized warfare. That's one reason I am such a go-between for Uncle Peter and the League, I am making votes for my man, so I consider it all right for me never to deliver any of their messages to each other as they are given to me, but to twist them into agreeability to suit myself.

Sallie said the Dominie was entirely on our side and that was why she went walking with him Sunday afternoon. All the other men were cool to him and he is so sensitive.

But to get back to the back yard. I glory in writing it and want the Five to consider it as almost sacred data, though I hope they will never have to do likewise.

Jane and Nell and Aunt Augusta took the two axes and one large hammer and tore down my back fence while I and the others loaded the planks on the wagon. Jane appointed Henrietta to sit and hold the slow old horses in case they should have got demoralized by the militant atmosphere pervading Glendale and try to bolt. I never saw any human being enjoy herself as Henrietta did, and it was worth it all just to look into her radiant countenance.

Jane took all the hard top blows to do herself and left the unloosening of the lower nails to Aunt Augusta while Nell ripped off the planks that stuck. I could almost hear Nell's long, polished finger nails go with a rip every time she jerked a particularly tough old plank into subjection, and Aunt Augusta dispensed encouraging axioms about pioneer work as she banged along behind Jane. Jane herself looked as cool as a cucumber, didn't get the least bit ruffled, and had the expression on her face that the truly normal woman has while she is hemming a baby's flannel petticoat.

And though during the day many delightful crises were precipitated, the most interesting were the expressions that devastated Polk Hayes's and Lee Greenfield's faces as they came around the side of the house to see what all that hammering was about.

"Caroline!" exclaimed Lee, in perfect agony, as he beheld the lady of his ardent, though long-restrained, affections poised across the wheel of the wagon tugging at the middle of a heavy plank which Mrs. Dodd and I were pushing up to her, while Mamie, the mother of seven, stood firmly on top of the wagon guiding it into place.

"Help!" gasped Polk, as he started to take the ax from Jane by force.

Then we all stopped while Jane quietly gurgled the molasses of the situation to them, and sent them on down the street sadder and wiser men. I thought Polk was going to cry on her shoulder before he was finally persuaded to go and leave us to our fate, and the expression on Lee's face as he looked up at torn, dirty, perspiring Caroline, with a smudge on her nose and blood on her hand from an absolutely insignificant scratch, was such as ought to have been on Ned's face as he ought to have been standing by

Mamie with the asafetida bottle. That's mixed up but the Five ought to catch the point.

It took up all of Saturday afternoon and part of Monday morning, but we built those tables, thereby disciplining masculine Glendale with a severity that I didn't think could have been in us.

We all rested on Sunday, that is, ostensibly. Jane put down all sorts of things on paper that everybody had to do on Monday and on Tuesday. Henrietta sat by her in a state of trance and it did me good to see Sallie out in the hammock at Widegables taking care of both the Kit and the Pup, laboriously assisted by panting Aunt Dilsie, because Jane explained to her so beautifully that she needed a lot of Henrietta's time, that Sallie acquiesced with good-natured bewilderment. Of course, Cousin Jasmine helped her some, but she was busy aiding Cousin Martha to beat up some mysterious eggs in the kitchen - with the shutters shut because it was Sunday. It was something that takes two days to "set" and was to be the *piece de resistance*, after the barbecue.

Mrs. Hargrove couldn't help Sallie at all with the kiddies, either, because she was looking through all her boxes and bundles for a letter from her son, which she thought said something about favoring woman's rights, and if it is like she thinks it is, she is going to go to the barbecue and get things nice and hot instead of having them brought to her cold.

I had hoped to get a few minutes Sunday afternoon to myself so I could go up into the garret and look through one of the trunks I brought from Paris with me to see how many sets of things I have got left. I am going to need a trousseau pretty soon, and I might need it more suddenly than I expect. I don't see any reason for people's not marrying immediately when they make up their minds, and my half of ours is made up strong enough to decidedly influence rapidity in his. But then I really don't believe that the Crag would care very much about the high lights of a trousseau, and it was just as well that Nell came in to get me to help her write a letter to National Headquarters to know if she could have any kind of assignment in the Campaign for the Convention to alter the Constitution in Tennessee when it meets next winter.

"Have you made up your mind fully to go in for public life, Nell?" I asked mildly. "Some of your friends might not like it very much and - and - "

"If you mean Polk Hayes, Evelina," Nell answered with the positiveness that only a very young person can get up the courage to use, "I have forgot that I was ever influenced by his narrow-minded, primitive personality at all. If I ever love and marry it will be a man who can appreciate and further my real woman's destiny."

"Well, then, that's all right," I answered with such relief in my heart that it must have showed in my voice and face. I had worried about Nell since I could see plainly, though she hasn't told me yet, and I am sure he doesn't realize it, that Jane had decided Folk's destiny. Nell is not twenty-one yet and she will find lots of men in the world that will be fully capable of making her believe they feel that way about her destiny, until they succeed in tying her up to using it for the real utilitarian purposes they are sure such a pretty woman is created for.

It will take men in general another hundred years yet, and lots of suffering, to realize that a woman's destiny is anything but himself, and get to housekeeping with her on that basis.

Of course, I see the justice and need of perfect equality in all things between the sexes, emotional equality especially, but I hope the time will never come when men get as hungry to see their women folks as said feminists get to see them, after they have been away about four days out in the Harpeth Valley. It takes a woman's patience to stand the tug.

The Crag didn't jog into Glendale on his raw-boned old horse until one-thirty Monday night. I had been watching down Providence Road for him from my pillow ever since I put out my light at eleven, because Jane had decided that it was our duty to go to bed early so as to be as fresh as possible for the rally in the morning. She had walked to the gate with Polk at ten and hadn't come back until eleven, so, of course, she was ready to turn in. It was just foolish, primitive old convention that kept me from slipping on my slippers and dressing-gown - I've got the prettiest ones that ever came across the Atlantic, Louise de Mereton, Rue de Rivoli, Paris - and going down to the gate to see him for just a minute. That second he stood undecided in the middle of the road looking at my darkened house was agony that I'm not going to put up with very much longer.

Scientifically I feel that I'm thinking life with one lobe of my brain and breathing with one lung. Still I made myself go to sleep.

Everybody believes in God in a different kind of way, and mine satisfies me entirely. I know that the hairs of my head are numbered and that not a sparrow falls; and I don't stop at that. I feel sure that my tears are measured and my smiles are rejoiced over, and when I want a good day to come to me I ask for it and mostly get it. There never was another like the one He sent me down this morning on the first slim ray of dawn that slid over the

Maria Thompson Daviess

side of Old Harpeth!

The sun was warm and jolly and hospitable from the arrival of its first rays, but the wind was deliciously cool and bracing and full of the wine of October. It came racing across the fields laden with harvest scents, blustering a bit now and then enough to bring down a shower of nuts or to make the yellow corn in the shocks in the fields rustle ominously of a winter soon to come.

The maples on the bluff were garmented in royal crimson brocaded with yellow, the buck-bushes that grew along the edges of the rocks were strung with magenta berries and regiments of tall royal purple iron weeds and yellow-plumed golden-rod were marshaled in squads and clumps for a background for the long tables.

Jane and I with Henrietta were out by the old gray moss rock at the first break of day, installing Jasper and Petunia and a few of their *confreres*. Jasper has always been king of all Glendale barbecue-pits and he had had them dug the day before and filled with dry hickory fires all night, and his mien was so haughty that I trembled for the slaves under his command. His basket of "yarbs" was under the side of the rock in hoodoo-like shadows and the wagons of poor, innocent, sacrificed lambs and turkeys and sucking-pigs were backed up by the largest infernal pit. Petunia was already elbow deep in a cedar tub of corn meal for the pones, and another minion was shucking late roasting-ears and washing the sweet potatoes to be packed down with the meat by eight o-clock. A wagon was to collect the baked hams and sandwiches and biscuits and confections of all variety and pedigree from the rest of the League at ten o'clock.

We didn't know it then but another wagon was already being loaded very privately in town with ice and bottles, glasses and lemons and mint and kegs and schooners. I am awfully glad that the Equality League had forgotten all about the wetting up of the rally, because I don't believe we would have been equal to the situation with Aunt Augusta and Jane both prohibition enthusiasts, but it did so promote the sentiment of peace and good cheer during the day for us to all feel that the men had not failed us in a crisis, as well as in the natural qualities inherent in their offering for the feast. There was a whole case of Uncle Peter's private stock. Could human nature have done better than that?

But if we did forget to provide the liquids, I am glad we had the foresight to provide other viands enough to feed a regiment, because a whole army came.

"Evelina," gasped Jane, as we stood on the edge of the bluff that commands a view of almost all the Harpeth Valley stretched out like the very garden of Eden itself, crossed by silver creeks, lined with broad roads and mantled in the richness of the harvest haze, "can all those wagons full of people be coming to accept our invitation?"

"Yes, they're our guests," I answered, with the elation of generations of rally-givers rising in my breast, as I saw the stream of wagons and carriages and buggies, with now and then a motor-car, all approaching Glendale from all points of the compass.

"Have we enough to feed them. Jasper?" she turned and asked in still further alarm.

"Nothing never give out in Glendale yit, since we took the cover offen the pits for Old Hickory in my granddad's time," he answered, with a trace of offense in his voice, as he stood over a half tub of butter mixing in his yarbs with mutterings that sounded like incantations. I drew Jane away for I felt that it was no time to disturb him, when the basting of his baked meats was just about to begin.

I was glad that about all the countryside had gathered, unhitched their wagons, picketed their horses, and got down to the enjoyment of the day before the motor-cars bringing the distinguished guests had even started from Bolivar. It was great to watch the farmers slap neighbors on the back, exchange news and tobacco plugs, while the rosy women folks grouped and ungrouped in radiant good cheer with children squirming and tangling over and under and around the rejoicings.

"This, Evelina," remarked Jane, with controlled emotion in her voice and a mist in her eyes behind their glasses, "is not only the bone and sinew but also the rich red blood in the arteries of our nation. I feel humbled and honored at being permitted to go among them."

And the sight of dear old Jane "mixing" with those Harpeth Valley farmer folk was one of the things I have put aside to remember for always. They all knew me, of course, and I was a bit teary at their greetings. Big motherly women took me in their arms and younger ones laid their babies in my arms and laughed and cried over me, while every few minutes some rugged old farmer would call out for Colonel Shelby's "little gal" and look searchingly in my face for the likeness to my fire-eating, old Confederate, politician father.

But it was Jane that took them by storm and kept them, too, through the crisis of the day. Jane is the *reveille* the Harpeth Valley has been waiting for for fifty years. I thought I was, but Jane is it.

And it was into an atmosphere of almost hilarious

enjoyment that the distinguished Commission arrived a few minutes before noon, just as Jasper's barbecue-pits were beginning to send forth absolutely maddening aromas.

Nell whirled up the hill first and turned her Buick across the road by the bluff with that rakish skill of hers that always sends my heart into my throat. And whom did she have sitting at her blue, embroidered linen elbow but Richard Hall himself? Good old big, strong dandy Dickie, how great it was to see him again, and if I had had my own heart in my breast it would have leaped with delight at the sight of him! But even the Crag's that I had exchanged mine for, though it was an entire stranger to Dickie, beat fast enough in sympathy with the dance in my eyes to send the color up to my face in good fashion as I hurried across a clump of golden-rod to meet him.

"Evelina, the Lovely!" he exclaimed in his big booming voice, as he took me by both shoulders and shook me instead of shaking merely my hand.

"Richard the Royal!" I answered in our old *Quartier Latin* form of greeting. I didn't look right into his eyes as I always had, however, and something sent a keen pain through the exchanged heart in my breast at the thought that I might be obliged to hurt the dandy old dear.

But suddenly the sight of Nell's loveliness cheered me. She had had Dick in that car with her ever since nine o'clock, almost three hours, showing him the sights of that teeming heavy lush harvest countryside around Bolivar and Glendale, all over which are low-roofed old country houses which brood over families that cluster around the unit that one man and a woman make in their commonwealth. Nell's eyes were sweet as she looked at him. I'll wait and see if I need to worry over him. With the

Maria Thompson Daviess

fervor I felt I had a right to, I then avoided the issue of Richard's eyes, put it up to God and Nell, and introduced him to Jane.

And while the three of them stood waiting for Nell to back up the Buick and put her spark-plug in her pocket, - only Richard calmly took it and put it in his, - the rest of the cars came up the hill and turned into the edge of the golden-rod.

Aunt Augusta was in the first one with the Chairman of the Commission, whose name even would have paralyzed anybody but Aunt Augusta; and Mamie and Cousin Martha, Caroline and several more of the ladies made up the rest of the Committee who had gone to escort the distinguished guests to the rally.

The Crag was in the last car with a perfectly delicious old gray-haired edition of Dickie, and I almost fell on both their necks at once. What saved them was Polk appearing between us with three long mint-topped glasses.

I'm glad old Dick immediately had his eyebrows well tangled in the mint of his julep, for I got my own eyes farther down into Cousin James's deep gray ones than I expected and it was hard to come up. I hadn't had a plunge in them for three days and I went pretty deep.

"Eve!" he said softly, as he raised his glass and smiled across his green tuft.

Yes, I know he knows that I know, there is an answer to that name when he says it that way, but I'm not going to give it until I am ready and the place is romantically secluded enough to suit me. He just dares me when he says it to me before other people. That reminds me, the harvest moon is full to-night and rises an hour later every evening from now on. I don't want to wait another month before I propose to him. I've always chosen moonlight for that catastrophe of my life. I wonder if men have as good times planning the culmination of their suits as I am having with mine?

But I had to come down quickly to a little thing like the rally and give the signal to feed all the five hundred people, who by that time were nice, polite, ravening wolves, for Jasper had uncovered the turkey-pit to keep them from getting too brown while the lambs caught up with them.

Jane was the master of ceremonies, because I balked at the last minute. I think I would be capable of managing even a National Convention in Chicago - that far away from the Harpeth Valley, - but I couldn't do it with my friends of pioneer generations looking on. A man or woman never grows up at all to the woman who has knitted baby socks for them or the man who has let them ride down the hill on the front of his saddle.

And at the head of the center table Jane asked the Crag to sit beside her, so that he would be in place to command attention for her when she wanted to speak, and where everybody could hear him when he did.

And while the table was piled high and emptied, and piled high again, so many bouquets of oratory were culled, tied, and cast at the guests along the table that I believe they would have been obliged to pay exclusive attention to them if the things to eat had not been just as odoriferous and substantial. Before dinner was over everybody had spoken that was of a suitable age, and some that had heretofore in the Harpeth Valley been considered of an unsuitable sex.

Jane's speech of welcome made such an impression that it is no wonder some of the old mothers in Israel got up to iterate it, as the dinner progressed.

She, as usual, refrained from prejudice-smashing and stones-at-glass-houses throwing, and she hadn't said ten sentences before she had the whole feeding multitude with her.

She began on the way our pioneer mothers had to contrive to keep larders stocked and good things ready for the households, and she tickled the palate of every man present by mentioning every achievement in a culinary way that every woman of his household had made in all the generations that had gone over Harpeth Valley. She called all the concoctions by their right names, too, and she always gave the name of the originator, who was some dear old lady that was sleeping in the Greenwood at the foot of the hill, or in some grave over at Providence or Hillsboro or Bolivar, and who was grandmother or great-grandmother to a hundred or more of the guests. I had wondered why Jane had been poring over that old autograph manuscript receipt book in my desk for days, and as she paid these modern resurrecting compliments to the long gone cooks, tears and laughed literally deluged the table.

And as she built up, achievement by achievement, the domestic woman-history of the valley, Jane showed in the most insidious way possible how the pioneer women had been really the warp on which had been woven the woof of the whole history of their part of the Nation, political, financial, and religious. I never heard anything like it in all my life, and as I looked down those long tables at those aroused, tense, farmer faces, I knew Jane had cracked the geological crust of the Harpeth Valley, and built a brake that would stop any whirlwind on the woman-question that might attempt to come in on us over the Ridge from the outside world. They saw her point and were hard hit. When "Votes for Women" gets to coming down Providence Road the farmers will hitch up a wagon and take mother and the children with a well-packed lunch basket to meet it half way. This is a prophecy!

Then, after Jane sat down, I don't believe such a speechifying ever was before as resounded out over the river, even in the time of Old Hickory. Everybody had something to say and got to his feet to say it well, even if some of them did brandish a turkey wing or a lamb rib to emphasize their points.

And the women were the funniest things I ever beheld, as we were treated to one maiden speech after another, issuing from the lips of plump matrons anywhere from thirty to sixty. They had never done it before, but liked it after they had tried.

Mother Mayberry from Providence, who is the grand old woman of the whole valley, having established her claim to the title thirty years ago by taking up her dead doctor husband's practice and "riding saddlebags to suffering ever since," as she puts it, broke the feminine ice by rising from her seat by the side of one of the entranced Magnates, - who had been so delighted with her and her philosophies that he could hardly do his dinner justice, - and addressing the rally in her wonderful old voice with her white curls flying and her cheeks as pink as a girl's.

"Children," she said, after everybody had clapped and clapped so she couldn't get a start for several minutes, "The Harpeth Valley women have been a-marching along behind the men for many a day, because their strong shoulders had to break undergrowth for both, but now husbands and fathers and sons have got their feet up on the bluff of Paradise Ridge, and it does look like they will be a-reaching down their hands to help us up, in the break of a new day, to stand by their side; and I, for one, say mount! - I'm ready!"

A perfect war of applause answered her, and Dickie's father got up to go down the whole length of the table to shake hands with her, but had to wait until she came out of the embrace of Nell's fluffy arms, and got a hand free from the Magnate on one side and Aunt Augusta on the other.

Even Sallie began to look speechful, and I believe she would have got up and spoken a few words on the subject of women, and how they need men to look after them, but she said something to Mr. Haley, who shook his head and then got up and prosed beautifully to us for ten minutes, and would have gone on longer, if he hadn't seen Henrietta begin to look mutinous.

The feast had begun at one o'clock, but by Jasper's skilful maneuvering of one gorgeous viand after the other, into the right place, by having relays of pones browned to the right turn and potatoes at the proper bursting point, it had been prolonged until the shadows of late afternoon were beginning to turn purple.

"Don't nobody ever leave one of my barbecue tables until sundown begins to tetch up the empty bones," has been his boast for years. And as he had cleared away the last scrap from the last table, he leaned against a tree, exhausted and triumphant, with alert, adoring eyes fixed on the Crag, who had risen in his place at the head of the long central table.

I had felt entirely too far away from him down at the other end with one of the junior Magnates and Dickie, but I was glad then that I sat so I could look straight into his face as the light from across the Harpeth Valley illumined it without, while a wonderful glow lit it from within.

All of the others had spoken of the achievements of their families and forefathers and vaunted the human history of the valley, but he spoke of the great hill-rimmed Earth Pocket itself. He gave the Earth credit for the crops that she had yielded up for her children's sustenance. He described how she had bred forest kings for the building of their homes, granted stores of fuel from her mines for their warming, and nourished great white cotton patches and flocks of sheep to clothe them from frosts and winds.

And as he spoke in a powerful voice that intoned up in the tree-tops like a great deep bell, he turned and looked out over the valley with an expression like what must have been on Moses's face when he saw into the promised land.

"She's our Mother," he said, as he flung back the long lock from across his forehead and stretched out his strong arm and slender hand towards the sun that was dropping fast down to the rim of Old Harpeth. "She has bared her breasts to suckle us, covered us from sun and snow, and now she expects something from us. If she has built us strong and ready, then we are to answer when the world has need of us and her storehouses and mines. We are to give out her invitations and welcome all who are hungry and who come a-seeking. Gentlemen, her wealth and her fertility are yours - and her beauty!"

For a long, long minute every face in the assembly was turned to the setting sun, and a perfect glory rose from the valley and burned the call of its grandeur into their eyes. We seemed to be looking across fields and forests and streams to the dim purple hills that might be the ramparts of the Holy City itself, while just below us lay the little

Maria Thompson Daviess

quiet village of the dead whose souls must just have gone before.

And after that everybody rose with one accord and began to hurry to start out upon the long roads homeward, just as the great yellow moon rose in the east to balance the red old sun that was sinking in the west. Only the Magnate sat still in his place for several long minutes looking out across to Old Harpeth, and I wondered whether he was thinking about the Eternal City or how many rails it was going to take to span the valley at his feet.

And I - I just stood on the edge of the bluff by myself and let my soul lift up its wings of rejoicing that my Crag had got his beautiful desire for apostrophizing the Mother-Valley so all the world might hear. And then suddenly it came over me in a great warm, uplifting, awe-inspiring rush that a woman who takes on herself voluntarily the responsibility of marrying a poet and an orator and a mystic, who is the complete edition of a Mossback that all those qualities imply, must square her shoulders for a long, steady, pioneer march through a strange country.

Could such achievement be for me?

"Please God!" I prayed right across into the sunset, "make me a full cup that never fails him!"

I don't know how long I stood talking with God that way about my man, but when I turned and looked back under the maples everybody was gone, and I could hear the last rattle and whirl going down the hill. For a second I felt that there was nobody but Him and me left on the hill, but even in that second my heart knew better.

"Now?" I questioned myself softly, out over to the yellow moon that had at last languidly and gracefully risen, putting the finishing touch to the scene I had been planning for my proposal.

"Evelina," said the Crag quietly from where he stood leaning against the tallest maple, "shall we stay here forever and ever, or hurry down through the cemetery by the short cut to the station to say good-by to the railroaders as they expect us to do?"

Nobody ever had a better opening than that, and I ought to have said, "Be mine, be mine," with some sort of personal variation of the theme, and have clapped him to my breast and been happy ever after. That is what a courageous man would have done under the circumstances, with an opportunity like that, but I got the worst kind of scare I ever experienced, and answered:

"How much time have we got? Do you think we can make it?"

"Plenty," he answered comfortably as I began to quicken my pace to the little gate that leads between the hedge into the little half-acre of those who rest. Then as I tried to pass him, he caught my hand and made me walk in the narrow path close at his side.

Now even a very strong-minded woman, who had to go through a little graveyard with moonlight making the tombstones glower out from deep shadows of cedar trees, in the depths of which strange birds croak, while the wind rustles the dry leaves into piles as they fall, wouldn't feel like honorably proposing to the man she intended to marry, even if she was scrouged so close to his arm that it was difficult for both of them to walk, would she?

I excuse myself this time, but I must hold myself to the same standard that I want to hold Lee Greenfield to. How do I know that he hasn't had all sorts of cold, creepy feeling's keeping him from proposing to Caroline?

I hereby promise myself that I will ask Cousin James to marry me the next favorable opportunity I get, if I die with fright the next minute, or have to make the opportunity.

Still, I can't help wondering what does keep him so composed under the circumstances. Surely he wouldn't refuse me, but how do I know for sure? How does a man even know if a woman is - ?

CHAPTER X

TOGETHER?

When business and love crowd each other on a man's desk he calmly puts love in a pigeon-hole to wait for a convenient time and attends strictly to business, while a woman takes up and coddles the tender passion and stands business over in the corner with its face to the wall to keep it from intruding.

Dickie has been here a whole week since the barbecue-rally, ostensibly trying to get me down to making a few preliminary sketches for the gardens to his C. & G. railroad stations, and, of course, I am going to do them. I'm interested in them and I'm sensible of the honor it is to get the chance of making them: but the moon didn't rise until after ten o'clock last night and I'm getting nervous about that scene of sentiment I'm planning. I can't think of gardens!

Still, I am glad he stayed and that everybody has been giving him a party and that Nell is always there, for he hasn't had time to notice how I'm treating business and coddling -

Jane and Polk and Nell and Caroline and Lee and everybody else, including Sallie and the Dominie, have been all over my house all day and into the scandalous hours of the night, which in Glendale begin at eleven

Maria Thompson Daviess

o'clock and pass the limit at twelve, and I don't see how they stand so much of not being alone with each other. It is wearing me out.

I had positively decided on my own side steps for the scene of my proposal to the Crag, under the honeysuckle vine that still has a few brave and hearty blossoms to encourage me, with the harvest moon looking on, but moons and honeysuckle blossoms wait for no man and no woman especially. They are both fading, and I've never got the spot to myself more than a minute at a time yet. The Crag, with absolutely no knowledge of my intentions, except it may be a psychic one, sits there every night and smokes and looks out at Old Harpeth and maddens me, while some one of the others walks in and out and around and about and sits down beside him, where I want to be.

And as for the day time, I am so busy all day long, providing for this perpetual house-party, that I am dead to even friendship by night. Jane is doing over Glendale from city limits to the river, and I have to spend my time keeping the dear town from finding out what is being done to it.

She is hunting out everybody's pet idea or ideal for some sort of change or improvement to his, especially *his*, native town, and then leading him gently up to accomplishing it so that he will think he has done it entirely by himself, but will tell the next man he meets that there is nothing in the world like a tine energetic woman with good horse sense. In fact, Jane is courting the entire male population in a most scandalous fashion, and they'll be won before they know it.

"Now, that Confederate monument ought to have been built long ago out of that boulder from the river instead of hauling in a slicked-up granite slab that would er made the Glendale volunteers of '61 feel uncomfortable like they would do in the beds in the city hotels. Great idea of mine and that Yankee girl's - great idea - hey?" sputtered Uncle Peter, after Jane had spent the evening down with him and Aunt Augusta.

"It is a fine idea, Uncle Peter," I agreed with a concealed giggle.

"I've subscribed the first five dollars of the fifty for hauling, setting up and inscribing it, and we are going to let the women give half of it out of the egg-money they have got in that Equality Quilting Society - some kind of horse sense epidemic has broken out in this town, horse sense, Evelina, hey?" And he went on down the street perfectly delighted at having at last accomplished his pet scheme. He thought of it as exclusively his own by now, of course.

And the monument is just the beginning of what is going to begin in Glendale. Jane says so.

"There could be no better place than this rural community to try out a number of theories I have had in political economy as related to the activities of women, Evelina," she said to me to-day, looking at me in a benign and slightly confused way from behind her glasses. "Mr. Hayes and I were just talking some of them over to-night, and he seems so interested in seeing me institute some of the most important ones. How could you have ever thought such a man as he is lacking in seriousness of purpose, dear?"

"I feel sure that it was just my own frivolous streak that called out the frivolous in Polk, Jane dear," I answered with trepidation, hoping and praying that the inquisition would not go much further, and trying to remember just what I had written her about Polk.

"It may have been that," Jane answered, in a most naively relieved tone of voice. "But you don't know how happy I am, dear, to see that that streak is only an occasional charming vein that shows in you, but that you are now settling down steadily to your profession. I feel sure that when these garden drawings are done, you and Mr. Hall will have found your correct places in each other's lives and it will be just a glorious example of how superbly a man and woman can work together at the same profession. Mr. Hardin and I were talking about it just last night out on the side porch, and though he said very little I could see how gratified he was at the honors that had come to you and how much he likes Mr. Hall."

That settled it, and I made up my mind that when the Harvest Lady left us to-night to sink behind Old Harpeth, she wasn't going to leave me weakly lonesome. She doesn't set until two o'clock, and I'm going to take all the time I need.

And as serious and solemn as I feel over taking such a step for two as I am deciding on, I can't help looking forward to scribbling a terse and impersonal account of my having proposed to the man of my choice in this strong-minded book, adding a few words of sage advice for the Five, locking it and handing it, key and all, to Jane with a dramatic demand that she put her hundred thousand dollars in the Trust Company and begin to choose the Five from those she has had in mind.

Then before she has had time to read it, I am going to sneakily get it back and blot or tear out some of the things I have written. I can decide later what will be data and what will be dangerous to the cause.

"And you will be glad to have me - come and live for a time in your home life, dear?" Jane recalled me to the question in hand by saying wistfully. "I feel that I have never had such good friends before, anywhere, as these of yours are to me, Evelina," she added.

That's one time I got Jane completely in my arms and showed her what a really good hugging means south of Mason and Dixon's line. From later developments I am glad she had that slight initiation. It must have been serviceable to her New England disposition.

Then just as I was going to ask some of the plans she - and Polk - had made, over came Cousin Jasmine, with Cousin Annie and Mary, with Mrs. Hargrove puffing along behind them. They had come to see Jane, but I was allowed to stay and have my breath knocked out by their mission.

It seems Jane had got a great big book from some firm in New York that tells alt about herb-growing, and how difficult it is to get the ones needed for condiments and perfumes, and offering to buy first-class lavender and thyme and bergamot and sweet fern and things of that kind in any quantities at a good price. She had shown it to the little old ladies who had been secretly grieving at the separation from their garden out on their poorly rented farm, and the leaven had worked - on Mrs. Hargrove also. They go back to the farm and she with them! She had decided on raising mint to both dry and ship fresh, because he of the gay pajamas always liked to have it strong and fresh for the julep of his ancestors. I hope she won't forget to take that pattern of Japanese extraction with her and make some for the Crag now and then, for it will save my time. Horrors!

"We have fully decided on our course of action, Jane, and

Maria Thompson Daviess

Evelina, dears," said Cousin Jasmine in a positive little manner that she would have been as incapable of a month ago, as is a pet kitten of barking at the family dog, "but we do so dread to break it to dear James, because we feel that he may think we are not happy under his roof and be distressed. Do you believe we shall be able to make him see that we must pursue our independent life, though always needing the support of his affection and interest?"

"I believe you will, Cousin Jasmine," I said, wanting to both laugh and cry to see the Crag's burdens begin to roll off his shoulders like this. And the tears that didn't rise would have been real ones, too, for I found that, down in the corner of my heart, I had adored the picture of my oak with the tender little old vines clinging around him. It was the producing gourd I had most objected to and I couldn't see but she would be there until I unclasped her tendrils.

But I was forgetting that, in the modern theory of thought-waves, it is the simplest minds that get the ripples first and hardest. Sallie came over just as soon as the other delegation had got home to take the twins off her hands. Jane had gone upstairs to make more calculations on our reconstruction, and I was trying to get a large deep breath.

"Evelina." she said, as she sank in a chair near me and fastened her large, very young-in-soul, eyes on mine, "were you just joking Nell, or did you mean it, when you said the other day that you thought it would be cowardly of a woman not to show a man that she loved him, if he for any reason was not willing to make the first advances to her?" Sallie is perfectly lovely in the faint lavender and pink things that Jane made her decide to get in one conversation, whereas while Nell and Caroline and I had been looking up and bringing her surreptitious samples of all colors from the store all summer.

"Well, I don't know that I exactly meant Nell to take it all to heart," I answered without the slightest suspicion of what was coming. "But I do think, Sallie, it would be no more than honest, fearless, and within a woman's own greater rights."

"Mr. Haley was saying the other evening that a woman's sweet dependence was a man's most precious heritage," Sallie gently mused out on the atmosphere that was beginning to be pretty highly charged.

"Doesn't a woman have to depend on her husband's tenderness and care all of the time - time she is bearing a child, Sallie, even up to the asafoetida spoon crisis?" I asked with my cheeks in a flame but determined to stand my ground. "It does seem to me that nature puts her in a position to demand so much support from him in those times that she ought to rely on herself when she can. Especially as she is likely to bring an indefinite number of such crises into their joint existence."

Sallie laughed, for she remembered the high horse I had mounted on the subject of Mamie and Ned Hall the day after the Assembly dance.

And as I laughed suddenly a picture I had seen down at the Hall's flashed across my mind. I had gone down to tell Mamie something Aunt Augusta wanted her to propose next day at a meeting of the Equality League about drinking water in the public school building. Mamie has learned to make, with pink cheeks and shining eyes, the quaintest little speeches that always carry the house - and even made one at a public meeting when we invited the men to hand over our fifty dollars for the monument. Ned's face was a picture as he held a ruffle of her muslin gown between his fingers while she stood up to do it.

But the picture that flashed through my mind was dearer than that and I put it away in that jewel-box that I am going to open some day for my own man.

Both Mamie's nurse and cook had gone to the third funeral of the season and Mamie was feeding the entire family in the back yard. The kiddies were sitting in a row along the top of the back steps, eating cookies and milk, with bibs around their necks, - from the twelve year old Jennie, who had tied on hers for fun, down to the chubbykins next to the baby, - and Mamie was sitting flat on the grass in front of them nursing little Ned, with big Ned sitting beside her with his arm around both her and the baby. He was looking first down into her face, and then at the industrious kiddie getting his supper from the maternal fount, and then at the handsome bunch on the steps, as he alternately munched a bite of his cookie and fed Mamie one, to the delight of the children. The expression on his face as he looked at them, and her, and ate and laughed, is what is back of all that goes to make the American nation the greatest on earth. Amen!

"Sallie," I said, as I reached out and took her plump white hand in mine, "our men are the most wonderful in the world and they are ours any way we get them. They don't care how it is done, and neither do we, just so we belong in the right way."

"Then you don't think it would be any harm for me to tell Mr. Haley I think I could live on eighteen hundred dollars a year, until he gets sent to a larger church?" was the bomb that, thus encouraged, Sallie exploded in my face.

I'm awfully glad that I didn't get a chance to answer, for I don't want to be responsible for the future failure or success of Mr. Haley's ministry. Just then Henrietta burst into the room with the Kitten in her arms.

"Keep her for me, Evelina, please, ma'am," she said, with the dearest little chuckle, but not forgetting the polite "please," which Jane had had to suggest to her just once. What you've done for that wayward unmanageable genius of a child, Jane dear, makes you deserve ten of your own. That is - help!

"Cousin Augusta and Nell and Dickie and me is a going out to watch the man put the dyn'mite in the hole to blow the creek right up and Glendale, too, so they can see if they is enough clean water to put in the waterworks," she continued to explain. "Nell is a-going to take Dickie in her car, and Cousin Augusta is a-going to take me and Uncle Peter in her buggy. Dilsie have got the Kit and Cousin Marfy is a-watching to see she don't do nothing wrong with her. Oh, may I go, Sallie? Jane said I must always ask you."

"Yes, dearest," answered Sallie, immensely flattered by the deference thus paid her.

"How wonderful an influence the little talks Mr. Haley has had with Henrietta have had on her," she said, with such a happy glow on her face as the reformed one departed that I succeeded in suppressing the laugh that rose in me at the memory of Henrietta's account of the first one of the series.

Men need not fear that the time will ever come when they will cease to get the credit for making Earth's wheels go around, from the female inhabitants thereof. So I smiled to myself and buried my face in the fragrance under the bubbly Puppy girl's chin and coaxed her arms to clasp around my neck.

They are the holy throb of a woman's life - babies. Less than ten wouldn't satisfy me unless well scattered in ages,

Jane. On some questions I am not modern.

"Still I do feel so miserable leaving Cousin James so alone all winter," Sallie continued with the most beautiful sympathy in her voice, as she looked out of the window towards Widegables. "I wonder if I ought to make up my mind to stay with him? He loves the children so, and you know the plans of Cousin Jasmine and the others to go back to their farm."

"But he'll have his mother left," I said quietly but very encouragingly. I seemed to see the little green tendril that had unclasped from the oak turning on its stem and winding tight again.

"Miss Mathers was encouraging Cousin Martha to go to Colorado to see Elizabeth and her family for a long visit this winter. She hasn't seen Elizabeth since her mother died and she was so much interested in the easy way of traveling these days, as Miss Mathers described it, that she asked her to write for a time-table and what a ticket costs, just this morning. I really ought not to desert Cousin James."

"But think how lonely Mr. Haley is down in the parsonage and of his influence on Henrietta," I urged.

"Yes, I do feel drawn in both ways," sighed the poor tender gourd. "And then you will be here by yourself, so you can watch over Cousin James, as much as your work will allow you, can't you, Evelina?"

"Yes, I'll try to keep him from being too much alone," I answered with the most deceitful unconcern.

"I see him coming to supper and I must go, for I want to be with him all I can, if I am to leave him so soon. I may not make up my mind to it," with which threat Sallie departed and left me alone in the gloaming, a situation which seems to be becoming chronic with me now.

If I had it, I'd give another hundred thousand dollars to the cause, to hear that interview between Sallie and the Dominie. I wager he'll never know what happened and would swear it didn't, if confronted with a witness.

And also I felt so nervous with all this asking-in-marriage surging in the atmosphere that it was with difficulty that I sat through supper and listened to Jane and Polk, who had come in with her, plan town sewerage. To-morrow night I knew the moon wouldn't rise until eleven o'clock, and how did I know anyway that Sallie's emancipation might not get started on the wrong track and run into my Crag? His chivalry would never let him refuse a woman who proposed to him and he'll be in danger until I can do it and tell the town about it.

Jane and Polk had promised Dickie and Nell to motor down Providence Road as far as Cloverbend in the moonlight, and I think Caroline and Lee were going too. Polk looked positively agonized with embarrassed sorrow at leaving me all alone, and it was with difficulty that I got them off. I pleaded the greatest fatigue and my impatience amounted to crossness.

After they had gone I dismissed Jasper and Petunia and locked the back doors, put out all the lights in the house and retired to the side steps, determined to be invisible no matter who called - and wait!

And for one mortal hour there I sat alone in that waning old moonlight, that grew colder and paler by the minute, while the stiff breeze that poured down from Old Harpeth began to be vicious and icy as it nipped my ears and hands and nose and sent a chill down to my very toes.

Nobody came and there I sat!

Finally, with the tears tangling icily in my lashes, I got up and went into the house and lighted the fat pine under the logs in the hall. They had lain all ready for the torch for a whole year, just as I had lain for a lifetime until a few weeks ago. Then suddenly they blazed - as I had done.

My condition was pitiable. I felt that all nature had deserted me, the climate, Indian summer, the harvest moon and my own charm, but my head was up and I was going to crackle pluckily along to my blaze, so I turned towards the door to go across the road and put my fate to the test, even if I took pneumonia standing begging at his front door. I hoped I would find him in the lodge and -

"Evelina," he exclaimed as he burst open my door, flung himself into the firelight and seized my arm like a robber baron of the Twelfth Century, making a grab for his lady-love in the midst of her hostile kindred, "I thought I would never get here! I ran all the way up from the office. Here's a telegram from Mr. Hall that says that the two roads have merged and will take the bluff route past Glendale, and give us the shops, - and wants to appoint me the General Attorney for the Southern Section. They want me to come on to New York by the first train. Can you marry me in the morning so we can take the noon express from Bolivar? I won't go without you. Please, dear, please," and as he stood and looked at me in the firelight, all the relief and excitement over his news died out of his lovely eyes and just the want of me filled them from their very depths.

For several interminable centuries of time I stood perfectly still and looked into them daringly, drinking my fill for the first time and offering him a like cup in my own.

"Eve," he said so softly that I doubt if he really spoke the word.

"Adam!" I let myself go, and at last pressed my answer against his lips as he folded me tight and safe.

It must have been some time after, I am sure I don't know how long, but I was most beautifully adjusted against his shoulder and he had my hand pressed to his cheek, when the awfulness of what had happened brought me straight up on my own feet and almost out of his arms.

"Oh, how could you have done it!" I fairly wailed, as I thought of what this awful complication was going to lose for the Five to whom I felt more tender in that second than I had ever felt before.

"Done what?" he demanded in alarm, pressing both my hands against his breast and drawing me towards him again.

"Asked me to marry you when I - "

"I have been fighting desperately to see some way to offer myself and all my impedimenta to you all this time, and this has made it all right, don't you see, dear?" he interrupted me to say, as he took possession of me again and held me with a tender fierceness, which had more of suffering in it than passion. "I have always wanted you, Eve, since before you went away, but it didn't seem right to ask you to come into a life so encumbered as mine was. Poverty made it seem impossible, but now, if you will be just a little patient with them all, I can arrange - "

Maria Thompson Daviess

"I was going to arrange all that my own self, and now just see what you have done to me and a whole lot of other women, besides making me miserable all summer," and crowded so close under his chin that he couldn't see my face, I told him all about the tinder-box Jane had loaded and then set me on the lid to see that it exploded.

I had just worked myself up to the point of how my incendiary mission was about to touch off all the other love affairs in town, when he began to shake so with disrespectful laughter that I felt that my dignity was about to demand that I withdraw coldly from his arms, where I had just got so warm and comfortable and at home; but with the first slight intimation of my intention, which was conveyed by a very feeble indeed loosening of my arms from around his Henry Clay collar, he held me firmly against him and controlled his unseemly mirth, only I could still feel it convulsing his left lung, - though as I had no business being near enough to notice it, I felt it only fair not to.

"Please don't worry about those other Five dear women," he begged, in the nicest and most considerate voice possible so that I tightened my arms again as I listened. "If Miss Mathers doesn't feel justified in giving up the dowries by your - your failure to prove the proposition, we can just invite them all down here and in Glendale and Bolivar and Hillsboro and Providence, to say nothing of the countryside, we can plant them all cozily. I can delicately explain to their choices exactly how to let them manage circumstances like - " he illustrated his scheme just here until it took time for me to get breath to listen to the rest of his apology - "this and there is no telling, with such a start as the cult has got in the Harpeth Valley already, how far ft will spread. Please forgive me, dear!"

"Yes," I answered doubtfully. Then I raised my head and

looked him full in the face as I made my declaration calmly but with the perfect conviction that I still have and always will have, world without end. "Yes, but don't you think for one minute I don't *know* that what Jane and I and all the most advanced women in the world are trying for is the right and just and the only way for men and women to come logically into the kind of heritage you and I have stumbled into. Absolute freedom and equality between all human beings is going to be the price of Kingdom Come. I shall always be humiliated that I got scared out in the graveyard and didn't do it to you. It is going to be the regret of my life."

"Truly, I'm sorry, sweetheart," he answered most contritely. "If I were to take my hat and go back to the gate and come in again properly and let you do it, would that make you feel any better?"

"No, it wouldn't," I answered quickly because why should I be separated from him all the two and a half minutes it would take to play out that farce, when I have been separated from him all the twenty-five years that stretch from now back until the day of my birth? "I am going to bear it bravely and hold up my head and tell Jane - "

"I wouldn't bother to hold up my head to tell her, Evelina," came from the doorway in Polk's delighted drawl as he and Jane stepped into the room. "Pretty comfortably placed, that head, I should say."

"Oh, Jane!" I positively wailed as I extracted myself from the Crag's gray arms and buried myself in Jane's white serge ones that opened to receive me. And the seconds that I rested silently there Polk spent in shaking both of the Crag's hands and pounding him on the back so that I grew alarmed.

Maria Thompson Daviess

"I didn't do it, Jane, I didn't do it," I almost sobbed with fear of what her disappointment was going to be. "He beat me to it!"

"Truly. I'm sorry," Cousin James added to my apology as he stood with his arm on Polk's shoulder.

"I dare you, *dare*, you to tell 'em, Jane," Polk suddenly said, coming over and putting a hand on one of my shoulders and one on Jane's.

"Evelina and Mr. Hardin," Jane answered gallantly with her head assuming its lovely independent pose, but with the most wonderful blush spreading the beauty that always ought to have been hers all over her one-time plain face, "the wager stands as won by Evelina Shelby. She had properly prepared the ground and sowed the seed of justice and right thinking that I - I harvested to-night. I had the honor of offering marriage to Mr. Hayes just about fifteen minutes ago. I consider that mode of procedure proved as feasible and as soon as I have received my answer, whatever it is, I shall immediately proceed with making the endowment and choosing the five young women according to the agreement."

"Polk!" I exclaimed, turning to him in a perfect panic of alarm. Could he be trifling with Jane?

"Evelina," answered Polk, giving me a shake and a shove over in the direction of the Crag, "you ought to know me better than to think I would answer such a question as Jane put to me, while driving a cranky car in waning moonlight. If you and James will just mercifully betake yourselves out there on the porch in the cold for a few minutes I will try and add my data to this equality experiment with due dignity. Go!"

We went!

"Love-woman," whispered the Crag, after I had broken it to him that we were going to be a Governor of Tennessee, and not a railroad attorney, and he had crooned his "Swing Low" over me and rocked me against his breast for a century of seconds, down on my old front gate, "you are right about the whole question. I see that, and I want to help - but if I'm stupid about life, will you hold my hand in the dark?"

"Yes," I answered with both generosity and courage.

And truly if the world is in the dusk of the dawn of a new day, what can men and women do but cling tight and feel their way - together?

Maria Thompson Daviess

Choose from Thousands of 1stWorldLibrary Classics By

A. M. Barnard
Ada Leverson
Adolphus William Ward
Aesop
Agatha Christie
Alexander Aaronsohn
Alexander Kielland
Alexandre Dumas
Alfred Gatty
Alfred Ollivant
Alice Duer Miller
Alice Turner Curtis
Alice Dunbar
Allen Chapman
Ambrose Bierce
Amelia E. Barr
Amory H. Bradford
Andrew Lang
Andrew McFarland Davis
Andy Adams
Anna Alice Chapin
Anna Sewell
Annie Besant
Annie Hamilton Donnell
Annie Payson Call
Annie Roe Carr
Annonaymous
Anton Chekhov
Arnold Bennett
Arthur Conan Doyle
Arthur M. Winfield
Arthur Ransome
Arthur Schnitzler
Atticus
B.H. Baden-Powell
B. M. Bower
B. C. Chatterjee
Baroness Emmuska Orczy
Baroness Orczy
Basil King
Bayard Taylor
Ben Macomber
Bertha Muzzy Bower
Bjornstjerne Bjornson
Booth Tarkington
Boyd Cable
Bram Stoker
C. Collodi
C. E. Orr

C. M. Ingleby
Carolyn Wells
Catherine Parr Traill
Charles A. Eastman
Charles Amory Beach
Charles Dickens
Charles Dudley Warner
Charles Farrar Browne
Charles Ives
Charles Kingsley
Charles Klein
Charles Hanson Towne
Charles Lathrop Pack
Charles Romyn Dake
Charles Whibley
Charles Willing Beale
Charlotte M. Braeme
Charlotte M. Yonge
Charlotte Perkins Stetson
Clair W. Hayes
Clarence Day Jr.
Clarence E. Mulford
Clemence Housman
Confucius
Coningsby Dawson
Cornelis DeWitt Wilcox
Cyril Burleigh
D. H. Lawrence
Daniel Defoe
David Garnett
Dinah Craik
Don Carlos Janes
Donald Keyhoe
Dorothy Kilner
Dougan Clark
Douglas Fairbanks
E. Nesbit
E.P.Roe
E. Phillips Oppenheim
Earl Barnes
Edgar Rice Burroughs
Edith Van Dyne
Edith Wharton
Edward Everett Hale
Edward J. O'Biren
Edward S. Ellis
Edwin L. Arnold
Eleanor Atkins
Eliot Gregory

Elizabeth Gaskell
Elizabeth McCracken
Elizabeth Von Arnim
Ellem Key
Emerson Hough
Emilie F. Carlen
Emily Dickinson
Enid Bagnold
Enilor Macartney Lane
Erasmus W. Jones
Ernie Howard Pie
Ethel May Dell
Ethel Turner
Ethel Watts Mumford
Eugenie Foa
Eugene Wood
Eustace Hale Ball
Evelyn Everett-green
Everard Cotes
F. H. Cheley
F. J. Cross
F. Marion Crawford
Federick Austin Ogg
Ferdinand Ossendowski
Francis Bacon
Francis Darwin
Frances Hodgson Burnett
Frances Parkinson Keyes
Frank Gee Patchin
Frank Harris
Frank Jewett Mather
Frank L. Packard
Frank V. Webster
Frederic Stewart Isham
Frederick Trevor Hill
Frederick Winslow Taylor
Friedrich Kerst
Friedrich Nietzsche
Fyodor Dostoyevsky
G.A. Henty
G.K. Chesterton
Gabrielle E. Jackson
Garrett P. Serviss
Gaston Leroux
George A. Warren
George Ade
Geroge Bernard Shaw
George Durston
George Ebers

George Eliot
George Gissing
George MacDonald
George Meredith
George Orwell
George Sylvester Viereck
George Tucker
George W. Cable
George Wharton James
Gertrude Atherton
Gordon Casserly
Grace E. King
Grace Gallatin
Grace Greenwood
Grant Allen
Guillermo A. Sherwell
Gulielma Zollinger
Gustav Flaubert
H. A. Cody
H. B. Irving
H.C. Bailey
H. G. Wells
H. H. Munro
H. Irving Hancock
H. Rider Haggard
H. W. C. Davis
Haldeman Julius
Hall Caine
Hamilton Wright Mabie
Hans Christian Andersen
Harold Avery
Harold McGrath
Harriet Beecher Stowe
Harry Castlemon
Harry Coghill
Harry Houidini
Hayden Carruth
Helent Hunt Jackson
Helen Nicolay
Hendrik Conscience
Hendy David Thoreau
Henri Barbusse
Henrik Ibsen
Henry Adams
Henry Ford
Henry Frost
Henry James
Henry Jones Ford
Henry Seton Merriman
Henry W Longfellow
Herbert A. Giles

Herbert Carter
Herbert N. Casson
Herman Hesse
Hildegard G. Frey
Homer
Honore De Balzac
Horace B. Day
Horace Walpole
Horatio Alger Jr.
Howard Pyle
Howard R. Garis
Hugh Lofting
Hugh Walpole
Humphry Ward
Ian Maclaren
Inez Haynes Gillmore
Irving Bacheller
Isabel Hornibrook
Israel Abrahams
Ivan Turgenev
J.G.Austin
J. Henri Fabre
J. M. Barrie
J. Macdonald Oxley
J. S. Fletcher
J. S. Knowles
J. Storer Clouston
Jack London
Jacob Abbott
James Allen
James Andrews
James Baldwin
James Branch Cabell
James DeMille
James Joyce
James Lane Allen
James Lane Allen
James Oliver Curwood
James Oppenheim
James Otis
James R. Driscoll
Jane Austen
Jane L. Stewart
Janet Aldridge
Jens Peter Jacobsen
Jerome K. Jerome
John Burroughs
John Cournos
John F. Kennedy
John Gay
John Glasworthy

John Habberton
John Joy Bell
John Kendrick Bangs
John Milton
John Philip Sousa
Jonas Lauritz Idemil Lie
Jonathan Swift
Joseph A. Altsheler
Joseph Carey
Joseph Conrad
Joseph E. Badger Jr
Joseph Hergesheimer
Joseph Jacobs
Jules Vernes
Julian Hawthrone
Julie A Lippmann
Justin Huntly McCarthy
Kakuzo Okakura
Kenneth Grahame
Kenneth McGaffey
Kate Langley Bosher
Kate Langley Bosher
Katherine Cecil Thurston
Katherine Stokes
L. A. Abbot
L. T. Meade
L. Frank Baum
Latta Griswold
Laura Dent Crane
Laura Lee Hope
Laurence Housman
Lawrence Beasley
Leo Tolstoy
Leonid Andreyev
Lewis Carroll
Lewis Sperry Chafer
Lilian Bell
Lloyd Osbourne
Louis Hughes
Louis Tracy
Louisa May Alcott
Lucy Fitch Perkins
Lucy Maud Montgomery
Luther Benson
Lydia Miller Middleton
Lyndon Orr
M. Corvus
M. H. Adams
Margaret E. Sangster
Margret Howth
Margaret Vandercook

Margret Penrose
Maria Edgeworth
Maria Thompson Daviess
Mariano Azuela
Marion Polk Angellotti
Mark Overton
Mark Twain
Mary Austin
Mary Catherine Crowley
Mary Cole
Mary Hastings Bradley
Mary Roberts Rinehart
Mary Rowlandson
M. Wollstonecraft Shelley
Maud Lindsay
Max Beerbohm
Myra Kelly
Nathaniel Hawthrone
Nicolo Machiavelli
O. F. Walton
Oscar Wilde
Owen Johnson
P.G. Wodehouse
Paul and Mabel Thorne
Paul G. Tomlinson
Paul Severing
Percy Brebner
Peter B. Kyne
Plato
R. Derby Holmes
R. L. Stevenson
R. S. Ball
Rabindranath Tagore
Rahul Alvares
Ralph Bonehill
Ralph Henry Barbour
Ralph Victor
Ralph Waldo Emmerson
Rene Descartes
Rex Beach

Rex E. Beach
Richard Harding Davis
Richard Jefferies
Richard Le Gallienne
Robert Barr
Robert Frost
Robert Gordon Anderson
Robert L. Drake
Robert Lansing
Robert Lynd
Robert Michael Ballantyne
Robert W. Chambers
Rosa Nouchette Carey
Rudyard Kipling
Samuel B. Allison
Samuel Hopkins Adams
Sarah Bernhardt
Sarah C. Hallowell
Selma Lagerlof
Sherwood Anderson
Sigmund Freud
Standish O'Grady
Stanley Weyman
Stella Benson
Stella M. Francis
Stephen Crane
Stewart Edward White
Stijn Streuvels
Swami Abhedananda
Swami Parmananda
T. S. Ackland
T. S. Arthur
The Princess Der Ling
Thomas A. Janvier
Thomas A Kempis
Thomas Anderton
Thomas Bailey Aldrich
Thomas Bulfinch
Thomas De Quincey
Thomas Dixon

Thomas H. Huxley
Thomas Hardy
Thomas More
Thornton W. Burgess
U. S. Grant
Valentine Williams
Various Authors
Vaughan Kester
Victor Appleton
Victoria Cross
Virginia Woolf
Wadsworth Camp
Walter Camp
Walter Scott
Washington Irving
Wilbur Lawton
Wilkie Collins
Willa Cather
Willard F. Baker
William Dean Howells
William le Queux
W. Makepeace Thackeray
William W. Walter
William Shakespeare
Winston Churchill
Yei Theodora Ozaki
Yogi Ramacharaka
Young E. Allison
Zane Grey

* 9 7 8 1 4 2 1 8 2 3 4 4 7 *